Public Leadersh

M000306340

Designed to help midlevel and senior managers in organizations dedicated to public purposes, this book provides trained self-awareness to deploy values to guide decisions and build the culture of their organizations. The book explores how all managing involves leading and identifies the levels of ethical responsibility for managerial leaders.

Highlighting the fundamental role that ethics plays in organizational life, J. Patrick Dobel uses insights from cognitive and social psychology to discuss how to anticipate and address threats to integrity and value informed decision making. Building on traditional ethical theory and modern research, the book begins with the fundamental assumption that individuals possess responsibility when they act for ethical purposes and results in taking a position within a public or nonprofit organization. This assumption of responsibility recognizes the inherent discretion in all positions and claims that effective ethical management requires self-awareness, self-mastery, integrity and a working frame of one's values and character. The book pays special attention to the challenges of integrating diverse people and perspectives in public organizations as well as attending to the slippages to integrity in organizational life and how managers and leaders can foresee and address ethical slippage and corruption. The book provides checklists and decision frameworks that individuals can adopt and deploy to guide decisions.

Public Leadership Ethics: A Management Approach will help create strong value informed cultures supported by communication, transparency, incentives and strong management cadres to achieve high quality service and integrity-based actions. It will be of special interest to managerial leaders in public service and teaching in public administration and policy programs or executive training.

J. Patrick Dobel is Corbally Professor Emeritus in Public Service at the University of Washington. He teaches at the Daniel J. Evans School of Public Policy and Governance. His work studies the intersection of politics, institutions and judgment, and his teaching has covered strategy, leadership, public ethics and management. His main research explores the integration of values and institutional structure in articles such as "Holy Evil" and work on leadership legacy or political corruption. As an advisor on ethics and management, he has worked with many public and nonprofit agencies and served as the chair of various ethics commissions for King County and Seattle, Washington. He has authored several award winning articles as well as many others on public leadership, ethics and integrity in journals such as *The American Political Science Review*, *Public Administration Review*, *Administration and Society* and *Public Integrity*. His books *Compromise and Political Action: Political Morality in Liberal and Democratic Life* and *Public Integrity* are widely taught and study the reality of ethics in public life.

Public Leadership Ethics

A Management Approach

J. Patrick Dobel

Routledge
Taylor & Francis Group

LONDON AND NEW YORK

First published 2018 by Routledge

2 Park Square, Milton Park, Abingdon, Oxfordshire OX14 4RN
52 Vanderbilt Avenue, New York, NY 10017

Routledge is an imprint of the Taylor & Francis Group, an informa business

First issued in paperback 2019

Copyright © 2018 Taylor & Francis

The right of J. Patrick Dobel to be identified as author of this work
has been asserted by him in accordance with sections 77 and 78 of the
Copyright, Designs and Patents Act 1988.

All rights reserved. No part of this book may be reprinted or reproduced or
utilised in any form or by any electronic, mechanical, or other means, now
known or hereafter invented, including photocopying and recording, or in
any information storage or retrieval system, without permission in writing
from the publishers.

Notice:
Product or corporate names may be trademarks or registered trademarks,
and are used only for identification and explanation without intent to infringe.

Library of Congress Cataloging-in-Publication Data
A catalog record for this book has been requested

ISBN: 978-1-138-48547-1 (hbk)
ISBN: 978-0-367-46377-9 (pbk)

Typeset in Times New Roman
by Apex CoVantage, LLC

For Helena Woehler

Contents

Introduction

Ethics and Values

Ethics and values cover the standards of right and wrong and the personal qualities that support a person's ability to judge and act upon ethical norms. Ethical standards guide decisions and focus behavior for right or wrong action. They anchor a person's sense of personal and professional integrity. They also provide fundamental threads to weave together the narrative of personal identity and integrity that individuals use to define whom they are as persons.

Ethics and values are also embedded in qualities of character. These character virtues such as courage, conscientiousness, prudence and fidelity provide the emotional and cognitive dispositions and psychological foundation to focus attention, motivate and sustain good judgment and actions.

Every decision managers and leaders take in organizations involves ethics. The quality of life and welfare of people in and out of the organization are impacted by decisions ranging from hiring and firing, to demanding competence to listening and addressing the issues of uneven or disrespectful service. People's lives and the conditions of common welfare such as water quality, public health and delivery of needed services to vulnerable people are impacted day in and day out. The criteria of the decisions, the tenacity with which they are pursued, and the competence and accountability of their execution implicate the basic ethical integrity, norms and character of the managerial leaders.

The design of an organization, its incentive structures and above all its informal and formal patterns of culture are prime determinants of whether a government or nonprofit organization will sustain high performance informed by strong public values. Attention to building and sustaining value driven performance becomes even more important as the political environment throws up obstacles to action or throws up actors seeking to subvert the performance of a public organization. This focus upon public values and character provides a robust lens through which leaders can focus their personal and institutional attention to nurture value informed actions.

In the end the design, structures and culture depend for their sustained influence on the committed and relentless attention, decisions and actions of senior and midlevel managers and leaders. Individuals holding positions of responsibility throughout organizations carry the power and capacity to concentrate the trained judgment of personnel and hold persons accountable to achieve the mission of public and nonprofit organizations as stewards of broad public purpose.

This book develops a framework and language of ethical values and character that can help leaders and managers appreciate and articulate the importance of values and character in leading effectively and building strong organizational cultures. It provides an account to help managerial leaders train their judgment to attend to ethical aspects of decisions in all decisions. These frames can guide deliberation, judgment and assessment for managerial leading.

The book develops this approach by discussing: the role of ethics in organizations; the nature of public values and commitments; their role in building strong public and nonprofit organizations; the range of values needed; and the strategies, tactics and skills needed by leaders and managers to generate these values and behaviors. It analyzes the unethical and illegal behaviors and norms that can undermine public value driven organizations. It devotes particular attention to the tendencies that subvert judgment and undermine organizational integrity. The book identifies leverage points that leaders can focus attention on to avert these dangers. It underlines the obligation to build a positive value driven organization. It concludes by examining a coordinated set of mental models that can inform managerial leadership. This leadership seeks to develop value supported high performance organizations by integrating daily management into long-term commitment to norms as well as forging the power and resource foundations to sustain mission-based results.

This approach has been developed in cooperation with many executive programs and executive masters' students. The book builds upon the existing literatures on managerial ethics, organizational culture and social and cognitive psychology but is deeply rooted in traditional understandings of public ethics. The book is designed to help students, leaders and managers develop their self-awareness of leading and figure out how to integrate ethical and character commitments into the daily life of leading organizations in a manner consistent with high quality integrity and performance to serve the common good.

Role and Professional Ethics

Personal values, commitments and character provide the underpinning to make judgments and act upon them. Values and norms permit leaders and managers to visualize the direction they seek to pursue in their actions. Values provide the normative framework to evaluate situations, people and environments. They connect personal standards to the normative purpose of the organization's mission. Values are also a source of reflection and innovation as leaders imaginatively extend the reach of the values and authorizing standards.

Values connect with character and internal cognitive frames to inform perception, assessment and judgment. The connection of values with cognitive frames undergirded by emotional support and reflective appraisal provide the strength of character and persistence to both act upon the judgments and to adapt and learn from the impact of actions in the world. These mental models or frames operationalize integrity and ethics for professionals and managerial leaders.

Ethics at the middle and senior organizational level focuses on the standards and character required of individuals who hold positions of power and responsibility. In public purpose organizations, many of the standards are authorized or supported by law and undergirded by public power. Ethical duties arise when individuals take positions of authority within a web of accountability and command. Taking these positions means a person makes an explicit or implicit promise, sometimes oaths, to judge and act upon the standards imposed by law, the professional standards for a position and duties implied by the purpose of the organization. People agree to be accountable for those judgments and actions.

Holding a position of authority enmeshes a person in a web of obligations and dependencies. In a modern governance world, multiple institutions must collaborate to achieve common purposes that do not match any one jurisdiction's power or purview. In addition, leaders must weave common values and purpose across these collaborations and competing organizations. These tasks, along with multiple accountability paths, place even heavier burdens upon the ethics and character of managerial leaders as they must negotiate across these organizational domains and sectors but keep commitment and direction to achieve the organizational and policy goals.

Colleagues, superiors, peers, collaborators, vulnerable citizens, future humans and others rely upon people's consistent, competent and fair judgment and actions. If individuals in senior or middle roles fail, vulnerable personnel or citizens, or long-term public goods, can suffer serious consequences. Collaborations fall apart with lack of trust in each other or diffusion of purpose and organizational self-interest undermines common commitments. The legitimacy of the whole enterprises and joint actions can be undermined by failure of leading at this level. Allies, partners and collaborators who rely upon organizational actors keeping promises and delivering service and support can suffer grievous loss. Long-term and valuable relations of trust and support can be undermined. The responsibility to act with professional and personal ethics is even more important in an area where individuals possess special powers to deploy coercion or force in the performance of their duties or have great power over vulnerable clients such as teachers, public health officials or police officers.

Organizational Ethics and Values

While ethics and values often are identified as personal concerns, successful organizations create and sustain their own ethical standards of performance. The ethical culture of an organization becomes the operational ethics for most persons in the organization. This culture supports shared values and perceptions, commitment, identity and communication. An ethical culture informs and guides the cumulative actions of many connected persons in an organization and enables them to trust each other's judgment and promises. These cumulative actions guided by shared culture commitments give daily reality to the vision and mission of an organization.

Leaders and managers need to act in sustained manners over long periods of time to inculcate a strong culture of value driven decision making that survives the daily press of life. This defines value driven leading. The values reside in the norms of the culture and the widespread and accountable professional judgment of personnel. While senior leaders set the tone and vision, middle managerial leaders and supervisory personnel carry the norms of the organization and are the front-line of ethical performance, adaptation and culture.

Value Driven Leading

The book proceeds in Chapter 1 to examine the purposes and functions that ethics performs in public organizations. Chapter 2 examines the importance of managerial and leadership ethics as the driver and steward of the mission values and performance in an organization. Chapter 3 discusses how ethical judgment and action depend upon a concept of personal integrity. Personal integrity enables persons to become self-aware of their values and through reflective practice to integrate cognitive, emotional and physical activity that manifest as trained habits of judgment and action. The chapter also examines predictable and reoccurring organizational and cognitive threats to personal and professional integrity in organizations. Chapter 4 pulls forward these personal and organizational insights to identify high leverage areas that managers and leaders can focus on to build sustained ethical performance in an institution. Chapter 5 reinforces this approach by laying out the most important and referenced values that leaders need to remember and focus on, in themselves and others, to build mission driven organizations and policy. Chapter 6 returns to the reminders from Chapter 3 about how ethical and performance slippages occur in all organizations.

It maps out the most predictable and identifiable ethical wrongs that occur and presents a model to anticipate and invest leadership and managerial resources at critical points to prevent or engage unethical behavior and slippage in performance.

The concluding Chapters 7 and 8 bring together the ideas developed into a model of value driven leading and present four dimensions in a cognitive framework to guide decisions. A leader or manager with integrity needs to possess self-mastery that integrates their emotions, cognitions and perceptions. The importance of self-mastery and careful reflection builds on the personal responsibility that arises when persons take the initiative and lead. Here persons take control of themselves to align cognitive capacity to master values, character attributes, rules and goals. Each of the four dimensions generates a range of considerations that should inform a person's judgment.

Managerial leaders can train themselves to call up and work through these four dimensions to align their integrity and values with the institution's mission while accounting for organizational responsibilities to contribute to a long-term policy or culture. The model builds upon the values discussed in earlier chapters as well as the organizational and cognitive insights developed. This model and framework end with ensuring that leaders develop the resources and political support to create sustainable results. These four dimensions are:

- Understand one's values, character and mission commitment
- Manage the meaning of individual incidents or challenges
- Act to build organizational norms and policy direction
- Secure the power and resources necessary for resilient outcomes

These dimensions integrate the values and character attributes that the book analyzes as well as the models of organizational integrity and slippage into a cognitive process that focuses on individual perception, reflection and judgment to incorporate these aspects into a usable decision framework. This model or framework enables individuals to practice public virtue in their position by shaping their understanding and perception of situations through cognitive preparation and learning. This approach calls upon values and character as wellsprings of motivation as well as guides to decision making. Practicing the framework over time results in persons carrying cognitive frames in their minds. The frames guide them to concentrate attention and perception by attending to each dimension of responsible public leading.

The Appendices expand upon the approach of the book that encourages individuals to use the reflective space of self-awareness to call up a range of subject matters to direct their reflection. The appendices gather together the values, character, motivations and organizational insights on integrity and slippage into feasible behaviors. These behaviors point persons to doable actions that can be practiced and integrated into a managerial and leadership style that incorporates integrity and realism.

This book seeks to help individuals think through and guide their actions. It can be incorporated into training or teaching in management, leadership and policy. The book can supplement a management or leadership class or training or become part of a wider ranging ethics class. Either way the book builds a common language for understanding the range of ethical dimensions at stake in public and nonprofit organizations and how they can inform and strengthen managerial leadership.

This book grew from a decade long dialogue with my students in the Evans School Executive Master's Program. These discussions challenged me to distill the issues of ethics and responsible leadership into an approach that could be used by leaders who had to leave class and try to act with integrity the next day. My ideas evolved in exchanges with their honest and demanding dilemmas, questions and endless quests to return to their public and nonprofit organizations and lead with integrity and effectiveness. I owe them a profound debt of gratitude for their commitment to my learning as well as their own. The book gained immensely from the insights of the two outside reviewers. My special thanks to the crew at The Royal Drummer. The book would not have attained its final shape without unending discussions with my friends and colleagues Steve Page, Diana Gale, Sandra Archibald, Carole Jurkiewicz and above all Steve Smith. I hope this book can only match the passion and commitment of the many students, colleagues and friends who kept me growing in my teaching and writing. My final thanks, as ever, lies with my best friend and life partner—Lea, my love.

1 The Purposes of Ethics in Organizations

Organizations are designed to achieve results. These results implicate ethical consequences for both people inside and outside of organizations. Organizations with public purposes often are stewards of complex and necessary public functions and do not generate clear outcomes such as profit and loss. They serve long-term purposes and address issues that the private sector finds uninviting unless specific policy measures are taken. Public purposes and missions deepen the moral consequences of public purpose organizations and create high obligations to ensure competent, fair and effective results.

Strong and successful organizations build powerful cultures. The cultures of organizations carry the values that shape and justify the mission. The values are the carriers of ethical norms and character that suffuse the daily life of the organization. Cultures become more vital when public purposes are served since the organization cannot rely simply upon self-interest to motivate and achieve results.

The norms and character shaped by a culture support individuals and groups as they seek to achieve committed purposes against the predictable temptations of agents serving their own interests, subcultures pursuing their own interests or outside groups seeking to capture the public organization for their own purposes. The culture, if well designed and led, promulgates, socializes and imbeds the public purpose and commitment in the personnel pursuing public purpose results.

When these values and character attributes support strong cognitive frameworks that are internalized by personnel, culture becomes operationalized ethics for the people. Because organizations depend upon thousands of decisions made daily by many individuals in pursuit of common goals, having people share a commitment to shared values and aspire to ideals of character provides a strong foundation to support the daily decisions and actions of individuals. If supported by strong managerial leadership and well-designed incentives and structures, ethics becomes a fundamental resource of strong organizations and an obligation of good leaders and managers.

The Roles of Ethics in Institutions

- Anchors Integrity
- Focuses Discretion
- Identify and Address High Stakes
- Guards Institutional Legitimacy
- Carries Organizational Culture
- Informs Diversity and Respect

Anchors Integrity

Individual values and character ground decisions and express who people are. They are the means by which individual integrity aligns with an organization's mission. Values and character focus and guide decisions but also pervade and sustain the professional norms and values of the institution. Acting upon ethical values gives daily reality to the organization's vision and mission. Values and characters serve as the buttresses for the self-narration individuals develop to forge an identity. They are critical to asserting an ideal self, which becomes the internal reference for an individual's internal dialogue over correct decisions and sustained actions. These values become the self-reflective notation for selves as individuals navigate the challenges and tensions of keeping integrity in the face of endless tensions, compromises and decisions in organizational life. They become even more vital in assessing the consequences of action and asking whether the results actually comport with the valued purposes.

As the values and character are internalized by individuals, they buttress people against the standard and predictable pull of self-interested agents using the organization for their own purposes. This can include avoiding being accountable for mandated results and subverting accountability, as well as distorting performance for their own ends. These patterns exist in all organizations and require constant attention, oversight, accountability and alignment, where possible, with interests of personnel and above all institutional support for sustained professional integrity of the actors as they face these standard inclinations.

Ethics matters for persons and organizations because ethics both anchors and expresses integrity. People balance complicated lives and many duties and define selfhood by judgments and actions. Often people only learn what kind of human beings they are by deciding and acting in important situations. To do this well and sustain self-respect, individuals rely upon values and virtues to guide decisions and uphold selfhood in the long haul of work and life. Values and characters serve as major themes in the autobiographical narratives people construct to give coherence and worth to lives. These themes of personal identity and integrity enable individuals to direct actions in order to keep consistently to a sense of self.

Focuses the Use of Discretion

Ethics plays a critical role in public and nonprofit organizations because of its centrality to discretion. Discretion is fundamental to the act of managing and leading and means that individuals have a choice in responding to situations. Discretion pervades organizational life. Within the space of discretion lies the bias toward self-interested, self-protective or convenient actions. Ethics along with institutional design and oversight is one of the bulwarks to shore up discretion's connection with decisions consistent with the mission.

Senior leaders possess it as they work to set general direction and manage complex political and authorizing environments. Senior leaders must constantly make value driven decisions about priorities and directions for action. It comes into play at the middle and supervisory levels when rules fail to cover a situation, or several rules conflict, or acting upon seemingly clear rules would create significant harm. Every midlevel manager and line worker regularly face decisions about whether to attend to a problem, how to define the problem and decide upon actions from enforcement to guidance to reminding people. It comes to bear when new situations or surprises arise for which people have no agreed upon standard responses. In a diffuse power and shared governance world, leaders, managers and line personnel possess even more discretion as they must navigate the tensions of shared jurisdictions and incomplete accountability lines as well as gain cooperation and collaboration from partners and competitors in performing their obligations.

Identifies and Addresses High Stakes

Public and nonprofit organizations carry high responsibility for many major concerns from public safety to education to medical or homeless support to food or water security. They often serve future generations, vulnerable individuals or a common good that others may not devote time and attention toward such as safe food or water. Many decisions involve high stakes for the people dependent upon such agencies. The impact of these consequences upon the welfare of citizens and clients entails serious ethical stakes in many organizational decisions. Being clear about the ethical results of actions keeps people alert and aware of the serious nature of the jobs they pursue.

Day to day life can grind away at a sense of purpose or nobility of public or nonprofit public service. People grow tired and can forget not just the vital importance of the grant of responsibility of an organization but of how people rely upon the high-quality performance of their professional actions. Even when the organization or people forget or hide the true stakes of actions, personal decisions impact real people, the organization's culture and the welfare of citizens. Very often workers do not even see the impact of actions since they may serve in functional positions such as finance or human resources that support line operations. People may work on obscure or hidden obligations such as sewer inspectors, ensuring sanitary hospitals or water treatment that people do not see and take for granted.

These are the classic institutions whose success is unseen by people and underappreciated by the public, but the impacts of negligence are severe. In addition, normal psychological heuristics and tendencies to protect one's self-identity can encourage people to live in denial about the real impact of incompetent or lazy actions. Good managerial leaders keep the ethical norms and importance of actions alive in the minds of staff and personnel and manage in a way that models and reinforces high quality and consistent work commitment to performing even the hidden but vital ethical actions.

The legitimacy or economic well-being of a public purpose institution is won or lost by the daily unfolding competence and relational dynamics of people doing their jobs. Public welfare and services are built up by day-by-day actions structured and guided by managerial leaders. The quality of service is, in turn, influenced by leadership of managers and the quality of relations and beliefs among the workers doing the jobs. How individuals lead reacts back upon both the quality of internal relations as well as the quality of external impact and relations.

This reality means that public and nonprofit institutions are deeply vulnerable to ethical collapse and scandal. Their failures ripple out as lost legitimacy, which has ruinous consequences for government and nonprofits. More than one hopes for but less often than it seems in the media, public organizations collapse or get into serious ethical lapses due to thoughtless accretion of unexamined unethical actions. These actions harden as unseen but slowly impacting patterns that lead to disillusioned citizens or clients or disheartened coworkers who see corrupt or unethical patterns flourish unchecked.

The contagion effect of single actions over time can infect large portions of an institution or be segregated into certain areas. When this happens, competence is sacrificed. People underperform, and less service is provided for the resources expended. The lower quality or levels of service lead to accumulating social and economic deficits in the served areas. The values everyone wants to believe in get sacrificed for personal or institutional convenience, gain or to cover up a mistake.

This point of mission collapse can be hidden for a long time, and this aggravates the decline of the culture and increases the number of individuals who are involved either as participants or who collude by looking the other way. When the tipping point is reached or the corruption leaks into the media, this type of collapse both undermines the legitimacy of the public and nonprofit sectors, and it hurts the present and future citizens who depend on strong regulation and honest, competent service.

Any organization in the public eye can be a flash point for media coverage and scandals. These media frenzies destroy careers, undermine a program for years and hurt the legitimacy of the program, institution and sector. This reality imposes special obligations upon managerial leaders to examine their organizational worlds to anticipate and address failures of ethical performance before they reach the turning points. Attention to ethics and mission can cut through the bureaucratic self-interest and rationalizations to get to the core values and core issues that can be lost in the fog of daily turf battles and political friction.

Guards Institutional Legitimacy

Organizational legitimacy and trust remain fundamental attributes of any successful public organization, and ethics is central to maintaining legitimacy in the eyes of the general public. All over the world, public institutions are struggling to earn the trust and respect of the general public. In addition, nonprofit institutions depend upon their legitimacy as their main form of social capital. Trust enables a nonprofit to raise funds and be chosen over other competing good causes. Trust and legitimacy can minimize resistance to organizational decisions and lead to less enforcement and higher efficacy. Lawsuits, scandals, public failures and media frenzies all erode the legitimacy and trust people have for government or nonprofit organizations.

Decreased legitimacy increases evasion of the law, increases levels of illegal activity, increases resistance to enforcement and decreases normal compliance and even commitment to public-spirited laws and regulations. Decreased trust and respect for government hurts the ability to recruit people, raise funds or pursue organizational missions without excessive legal regulation. Lack of trust in public organizations increases resistance to taxes as well as compliance with laws. At the same time, decreased trust and respect warrant the public and clients to distrust public officials more and treat personnel with less respect, leading to a vicious cycle of public disdain engendering less respect and service from beleaguered officials.

Senior leaders need to make building legitimacy and trust for public institutions a fundamental part of their ethical leadership principles. Establishing legitimacy for the institution and projects emerges as vital in the world of governance and collaboration, where it becomes a continuous responsibility to shore up common purpose and demand mutual accountability across institutions. The legitimacy of the project depends not just upon public perceptions and results but also upon the shared commitment of the collaborators. It involves intense attention to financial stewardship, competence and efficiency to reassure people that money is well spent for authorized purposes. Managers and supervisors embody the values and mission and hold the legitimacy of government and nonprofit institutions in their hands as the front-line agents of leading and management. They are the point of interaction where almost all the good is accomplished but where slippage can generate the greatest harm.

Carries Organizational Culture

Managerial leaders and supervisory personnel live where "the rubber hits the road" in ethical terms. They handle endless complex, difficult and recurring issues. Their decisions involve discretion balancing laws, rules and ethical values. Their actions can generate more problems or prevent serious problems from occurring. Their actions establish models for others to abide by and generate credibility or hypocrisy. The daily cumulative decisions of managers and supervisors create patterns of expectations for good and bad actions. They build the institutional culture of the agency.

This daily generation of the reality of ethics connects deeply to the ideals and mission of the organization. If significant slippage occurs internally or externally, the very ideals that justify the mission become sources of disdain, disempowerment and resistance to the organization and the broader purposes it embodies.

Each decision of a managerial leader defines the nature of a problem, sets a precedent, contributes to the long-term policy or culture and will impact the resource base or power of an organization or team. Day-by-day decision making, leading and managing build expectations and set norms for the personnel. They set, for good or bad, cognitive frameworks that lay the foundation for the cultural norms and expectations that peer workers share and enforce on each other. The relations among workers and between leaders and workers are created by the ethics of managerial leaders. Workers can internalize shared ethical values that create common understandings of what is right and wrong. These values reinforce a collective organizational identity. Building and sustaining these shared understandings of purpose and rightness is a critical aspect of ethics in organizations. It also builds social support networks and informal understandings that sustain personnel as they face the duress of obdurate problems, clients or opposition.

Decisions accrue over time and build up patterns just as coral reefs accumulate over time. Cumulative actions build the cultural structures of organizations. The leaders' commitment and actions on behalf of certain values will sustain those values, while indifference or looking the other way will permit corrupt values to flourish in both personnel and citizens who interact with the institution. Virtue and corruption can be imbedded as cognitive frames and habits over time; people start to do the right or wrong thing and the behavior becomes an ingrained frame of reference that is largely unquestioned.

A few unethical or illegal actions can infect others through contagion and become imbedded in pockets or subcultures in an organization almost without people noticing. The decisions and actions of managers and supervisors create and sustain norms that support frames of judgment and patterns of behavior. Their negligence permits pockets that undermine mission performance. Managerial leaders and supervisors have strong obligations to exercise vigilance to address these issues when they arise. They model and enforce standards that will become the reference points for personnel, citizens and clients alike.

Informs Diversity and Respect

Organizational ethics and culture depend upon inculcating reliable norms and character that sustain consistent performance across large numbers of people over time. Shared purpose and common understandings and mutual trust are central to the role ethics plays in organizations. Yet in a democratic or respectful world of public or nonprofit service leaders, supervisors and personnel regularly face differences among themselves and with the citizens and clients they serve. An organizational ethic must figure out a way to engage such diversity in a way that builds reliable, respectful and competent results for all people served.

Racial, cultural, ethnic, religious and gender differences engage all public and nonprofit institutions. They pose challenges simply because a public purpose organization has public obligations that involve a common long-term good that subsumes the differences for a long-term mission aimed at the present and future welfare of all. In addition, pervasive economic and social inequality compound power differentials among the people served. Any agency anchored to respect dignity in serving citizens and clients actively needs to include respect for diverse individuals and groups in their ethical culture. All these differences can create differential treatment within and outside the organization which violate the norms that give legitimacy to the public and nonprofit institutions. Even different professional affiliations within an organization can lead to conflict across groups or institutional silos in an institution committed to a shared purpose.

The differences among clients or citizens and agency personnel can aggravate on-going and often hidden inequalities and tensions. Too often such differences cause friction, abuse or perceived abuse between managers and personnel or between personnel and citizens. The pressures to succeed in professional actions or pressures to meet institutional or performance goals collide with the intractable reality of clients and resource limits. This confrontation generates pressures that erode the commitment and performance of the best personnel.

Good managers and supervisors possess the clear responsibility and challenge to integrate diverse people into cohesive teams. This involves active efforts to recruit and promote within the organization to lay deep moral foundations of equality and respect within its walls. They need to not just build the cohesive teams across the myriad differences among people, but they have to actively figure out how to ensure that all people, regardless of differences from the organizational personnel, are treated with respect and competence. Public organizational ethics drives leaders to head off potential internal and external conflicts and actively address the predictable tensions when deep social and class differences rub against each other. In the crush of daily conflict, managerial leaders must model and teach personnel how to navigate the never-ending tensions and possibilities that differences create in and across institutions.

Bibliography

Arendt, H. (1965). *Eichmann in Jerusalem: A report on the banality of evil.* New York, NY: Penguin.

Bailey, S. K. (1964). Ethics and the public service. *Public Administration Review, 24*(4), 234–243.

Bertok, J. et al. (2005). *Public sector integrity: A framework for analysis.* Paris, France: OECD.

Bolman, L. G., & Deal, T. E. (2011). *Reframing organizations: Artistry, choice and leadership.* New York, NY: John Wiley & Sons.

Bowman, J. S. (Ed.). (1991). *Ethical frontiers in public management: Seeking new strategies to resolve ethical dilemmas.* San Francisco, CA: Jossey-Bass.

Bruce, W. (2001). *Classics of administrative ethics.* Boulder, CO. Westview Press.

Bryson, J., Crosby, B., & Bloomberg, L. (Ed.). (2015). *Creating public value in practice: Advancing the common good in a multi-sector, shared power, no-one-wholly-in-charge-world.* Boca Raton, FL: Taylor & Francis Group.

Burke, J. P. (1986). *Bureaucratic responsibility.* Baltimore, MD: The Johns Hopkins University Press.

Christensen, C. M., Allworth, J., & Dillon K. (2012). *How will you measure your life?* New York, NY: Harper Collins.

Ciulla, J. B. (2003). *The ethics of leadership.* Boston, MA: Wadsworth.

Cohen, S., & Eimicke, W. (2002). *The effective public manager: Achieving success in a changing government* (3rd edition). San Francisco, CA: Jossey-Bass.

Cooper, T. L. (1987). Hierarchy, virtue, and the practice of public administration: A perspective for normative ethics. *Public Administration Review, 47*(4), 320–328.

Cooper, T. L. (2006). *The responsible administrator: An approach to ethics for the administrative role* (5th edition). San Francisco, CA: Jossey-Bass Publishers.

Crick, B. (1972). *In defence of politics* (2nd edition). Chicago, IL: University of Chicago Press.

Denhardt, K. G. (1988). *The ethics of public service.* New York, NY: Greenwood.

Dobel, J. P. (1999). *Public integrity.* Baltimore, MD: Johns Hopkins University Press.

Dobel, J. P. (2005). Managerial leadership and the ethical importance of legacy. *International Public Management Journal, 8*(2), 225–246.

Dobel, J. P. (2007). Public management as ethics. In Ferlie, E., Lynn, Jr., L. E., & Pollitt, C. (Eds.), *The Oxford handbook of public management* (pp. 156–181). Oxford, UK: Oxford University Press.

Fairhurst, G. T., & Sarr, R. A. (1996). *The art of framing: Managing the language of leadership.* San Francisco, CA: Jossey-Bass Publishers.

Finer, H. (1941). Administrative responsibility in democratic government. *Public Administration Review, 1*(4), 335–350.

Fleishman, J. et al. (1981). *Public duties: The moral obligations of government officials.* Cambridge, MA: Harvard University Press.

Frederickson, H. G. (1997). *The spirit of public administration.* San Francisco, CA: Jossey-Bass.

Gawande, A. (2010). *Checklist manifesto.* New York, NY: Penguin Books.

Goodsell, C. (2011). *The mission mystique: Belief systems in public agencies.* Washington, DC: CQ Press.

Goodsell, C. (2015). *The new case for bureaucracy.* Washington, DC: CQ Press.

Hart, D. K. (1974). Social equity, justice, and the equitable administrator. *Public Administration Review, 34*(1), 3–11.

Huberts, L., & Hoekstra, A. (Eds.). (2016). *Integrity management in the public sector: The Dutch approach* (pp. 146–158). The Hague: Bios.

Jackall, R. (1988). *Moral mazes: The world of corporate managers.* Oxford, UK: Oxford University Press.

Janis, I. L. (1982). *Groupthink: Psychological studies of policy decisions and fiascoes.* Boston, MA: Houghton Mifflin.

Janis, I. L., & Mann, L. (1977). *Decision making: A psychological analysis of conflict, choice, and commitment.* New York, NY: Free Press.

Jurkiewicz, C. L. (Ed.). (2015). *The foundations of organizational evil.* London, UK: Routledge.

Kahneman, D. (2011). *Thinking, fast and slow.* New York, NY: Macmillan.

Klein, G. A. (1998). *Sources of power: How people make decisions.* Cambridge, MA: MIT Press.

Klein, G. A. (2009). *Streetlights and shadows: Searching for the keys to adaptive decision making.* Cambridge, MA: MIT Press.

Korsgaard, C. M. (2009). *Self-constitution: Agency, identity and integrity.* Oxford, UK: Oxford University Press.

Kouzes, J. M., & Posner, B. Z. (2011). *Credibility: How leaders gain and lose it, why people demand it* (Vol. 244). New York, NY: John Wiley & Sons.

Light, P. (1995). *Thickening government: Federal hierarchy and the diffusion of accountability.* Washington, DC: Brookings Institution.

March, J. G., & Olsen, J. P. (2010). *Rediscovering institutions.* New York, NY: Simon and Schuster.

Martin, R. C. (Ed.). (1965). *Public administration and democracy.* Syracuse, NY: Syracuse University Press.

Moore, M. M. (1995). *Creating public values: Strategic management in government.* Cambridge, MA: Harvard University Press.

Nagel, T. (1978). Ruthlessness in public life. In Hampshire, S. (Ed.), *Public and private morality* (pp. 75–92). Cambridge, UK: Cambridge University Press.

Price, T. (2008). *Leadership ethics: An introduction.* Cambridge, UK: Cambridge University Press.

Pritchard, M. S. (2006). *Professional integrity: Thinking ethically.* Lawrence, KS: University of Kansas Press.

Rawls, J. (1971). *A theory of justice.* Cambridge, MA: Belknap Press of Harvard University Press.

Riordon, W. (1963). *Plunkitt of Tammany Hall.* New York, NY: Dutton.

Rohr, J. A. (1986). *To run a constitution: The legitimacy of the administrative state.* Lawrence, KS: University of Kansas Press.

Rohr, J. A. (1988). *Ethics for bureaucrats: An essay on law and values* (2nd edition). New York, NY: Marcel Dekker.

Rohr, J. A. (1999). *Public service, ethics and constitutional practice.* Lawrence, KS: University of Kansas Press.

Salomon, R. C. (1992). *Ethics and excellence: Co-operation and integrity in business.* Oxford, UK: Oxford University Press.

Schon, D. (1984). *The reflective practitioner: How professionals think in action.* New York, NY: Basic Books.

Selznick, P. (1957, 1984). *Leadership in administration: A sociological perspective.* New York, NY: Harper Collins.

Svara, J. H. (2014). *The ethics primer for public administrators in government and nonprofit organizations.* Burlington, MA: Jones & Bartlett Publishers.

Weber, M. (1958). Politics as a vocation. In Gerth, H. H., & Mills, W. W. (Ed. & Trans.), *From Max Weber: Essays in sociology* (pp. 77–128). Oxford, UK: Oxford University Press.

Wilson, W. (1887). The study of administration. *Political Science Quarterly, 2*(2), 197–222.

2   Managers Lead

Managers dwell at the center of ethical activity and integrity for organizations. Supervisors, midlevel managers and senior managers create the mission of the organization. Managerial action is inherently ethical. It entails consequences to the common good and impacts the people who depend upon the competent performance of an organization's tasks and mission. Managerial actions affect the lives of the people who work with them; the quality of life and personhood of an organization's people are deeply influenced over time by the tutelage of managers.

Some of the management literature draws a very bright line between leading and managing imbedding managers in routine rule-bound activity and promoting leaders to vision and mission articulation. The reality of ethical life in organizations is very different. Most managers must constantly lead, and good leaders require a deep capacity to manage. The continuum of skills and frames of judgment are closely linked. A managerial leader, whether at the line or senior level:

- Develops and motivates a shared purpose among people to achieve tasks
- Refines goals, communicates with personnel, listens and adapts to daily conditions in achieving the results
- Performs daily tasks of direction and improvisation as they adapt to fluctuations in the organizational environment
- Takes the initiative to identify and address challenges to the task performance and culture as well as manages relations among group members
- Helps identify talent and develop skills and potential among staff
- Continuously monitors the boundary of group performance and guides relationships across cooperating and competing groups inside and outside the agency
- Exercises vigilance about slippages in performance and integrity at individual, group and organizational levels

- Remains responsible for assessing results and initiates accountability to improve implementation in light of organizational mission
- Builds a store of power and resources to sustain organizational capacity and performance

This range of behaviors and responsibilities scales from being responsible for a small task team to working in a senior management group deliberating on strategy or a crisis. Good managers incorporate ethical responsibility and seamlessly integrate aspects of leading into managing.

Managers hold very difficult jobs. The jobs are imbedded in the official positions they hold. The positions exist in a web of accountability to processes, laws, regulations and rules. The positions authorize the standards for judgment and point to the range of responsibilities and actions that the manager should devote attention to. Managers serve as stewards of accountability. They attend to budgets and efficiency and ensure that people respect processes or enact complicated regulations and laws. Managerial leaders live in a world of discretion and help interpret complex and conflicting written mandates as well as both requiring and enabling people to meet complex goals in limited time with scarce resources and political constraints.

While shepherding people to accomplish tasks, individual managers try to embody the values and ensure outcomes align with the organization's mission. Local staff and contractors look to managerial leaders to model the behaviors and decision patterns that will guide their own actions. Very often managers, even if bound by an official position, take on much more responsibility and mediate between beleaguered personnel and demanding outcome requirements imposed by authorizers or funders.

At the same time, managers must work at the boundaries to cooperate with multiple internal and external actors from budget and human resource personnel to vendors or contracted service providers. They often need to remind partners and stakeholders of the deeper purposes that authorize and should limit and direct everyone's decisions. These managers support their people and build culture and teamwork to help personnel avoid being overwhelmed in the face of limited resources, high expectations, scrutiny and populations or wicked problems that do not respond to easy solutions.

Managers act through an endless flow of daily decisions, many made with little time for reflection. These decisions and managerial competence depend heavily upon managers and leaders developing strong and reliable cognitive frameworks. These embody ethical mission-based standards along with the self-awareness and emotional and physical robustness to decide, act and adapt as conditions and people change under the stress of work and environmental shifts. Good managerial leaders actively train themselves to incorporate mental models and frameworks that combine the values, goals and character of their position and professional task.

The value driven leading framework highlights the responsibilities of managers who lead. It asks persons to exercise the discipline to remain open to reflect upon their moral capacity and values and how these align with and propel the organization's mission. This self-awareness serves as an ethical backstop to the daily demands of decisions. The framework bids managerial leaders to see the flow of incidents and challenges as involving long-term ethical norms for the organization and unfolding policy. The value driven frame reinforces the realism of a good manager that resilient outcomes require attention to attaining power and resources to support the outcome over time and against opposition.

While performing this difficult balancing act, managers need to earn the trust and compliance of their personnel and peers and promote and protect a culture. These are the means by which managerial leaders encourage high performance and goal expectations.

At the same time, individuals must answer to and manage up to their senior leaders who have their own concerns and careers to worry about. Managerial leaders live at the intersection of a complicated and unrelenting web of relations, obligations and conflicts that ensnare their positions and responsibilities.

Managerial Responsibility

- Promise as the Moral Foundation
- Personal Responsibility
- Self-Awareness

Promise as the Moral Foundation

The dominant ethical standards for individuals exercising discretion derive from role ethics. Managers and leaders within an organization exercise their power and authority based upon the assigned roles and responsibilities within the broader umbrella of the organization's moral or legal legitimacy. The traction of the ethics of taking an official position flows from the moral importance of a promise. Individual managers and leaders connect their integrity to their position by a personal promise to abide by the requirements of their official position.

The very act of promising, which holds the organizational enterprise together, depends upon the values and character traits that will be discussed in later chapters. For instance, making this promise presumes several fundamental ethical capacities and values. A person needs to possess the self-awareness or knowledge to be aware of what a position asks of them. They need the capacity to understand and then assess their own ability in terms of values, skills and temperaments to live up to the demands and responsibilities of the position.

Making a self-conscious pledge when taking the position entails possessing the conscientiousness, fidelity and courage to understand and live up to the standards of a position. Managers need the self-mastery to overcome internal temptations for careerist or self-interested actions. They commit to make the decisions and pursue actions in the face of any obstacles or challenges. The promise presumes the capacity for self-reflection and courage to avoid the pitfalls of social pressure and self-deception that accumulate from pressures in organizations to undermine mission commitment. Because the positions are imbedded in legal structures that are authorized to act for purposes, then the person making the promise involves not just skill and performance but the honesty, courage and openness to report and be accountable for actions.

Individuals take on a position within an organization and that position possesses an articulate set of responsibilities and accountability. But the position also warrants the person with the power to assign tasks, assess and direct people, allocate resources for different priorities and assess and change results to align with their judgments. This authority and power over people and resources creates a set of powerful responsibilities that impact human beings and long-term conditions of the world.

People who take these positions make a promise to judge within a framework of professional, legal and stewardship standards that instill accountability into the judgments. The promise also covers respecting the reporting standards, processes and transparency that sustain the legitimacy of the position and institution. The promise entwines a person's moral responsibility with actions performed under the warrant of the position. Without this promise, the entire edifice of democratic and organizational accountability breaks down.

Personal Responsibility

Making this promise means that the individual managers accepts personal responsibility for their actions. They make the position theirs. In theory and practice, managers may often seem to be simply enforcing the rules almost like automatons; in fact, every manager or leader brings their unique style, gifts and judgment to their role. Managers are not embodied algorithms. The position bonded by a promise connects to the leader's personal narrative and sense of ideal self, which they use to monitor and organize their emotions, thinking and actions.

The identical job in the same place and at the same time can be done in very different ways by two individuals both claiming simply to be "enforcing the rules." The outcomes may, in fact, be the same, but the process, style and cultural impact will be very different. The realities of personal style and judgment pervade managerial life and highlight the individual responsibility of leaders. This uniqueness of style and input provide one of the strongest foundations for understanding how leading and individuality link.

The results of managerial leading involve not just the outcome of a particular incident or action but the cumulative collateral effects on the quality and competence of personnel and the slow creation of a culture among people. This means responsibility inheres in leading and managing. It also underscores that there are many ways to lead effectively and that persons can engage challenges from multiple frameworks, find their own unique voice and still lead with ethics and accountability. This uniqueness can be a source of slippage itself but also defines the intersection where much necessary invention and innovation occurs in organizational tasks.

Personal responsibility and integrity become even more vital in a world where multiple organizations and jurisdictions must cooperate to achieve goals. Dealing with opposition and addressing partners, cooperators and collaboration challenges places heavy emphasis upon the ability of managerial leaders to take initiative and work with different actors. Such leaders are often needed to forge common understandings and purpose without reliance upon a single chain of authority or accountability. Individual managerial leaders must rely heavily upon personal integrity and judgment to make sense of the multiple lines of accountability and multiple organizational missions. They will need to improvise in such an open and muddled political space to weave together a shared understanding of goals and some mutual accountability. The personal responsibility of managerial leading authorizes individuals to exercise ethical initiative and imagination in achieving organizational purposes.

Self-Awareness

The central importance of personal responsibility and integrity to ethical managerial leadership depends upon the capacity for reflective self-awareness. The book will return to this aspect several times. The ability to stand back and become aware of one's situation, one's consequences of actions and one's ability to grapple with aligning organizational actions with values and character is fundamental to keep personal integrity intact. Without it, the power to make and keep promises erodes. Self-reflection enables a person to claim, assess and recalibrate their life and decisions. In classical philosophical terms, self-awareness merges with self-knowledge, which is the foundation of Western approaches to ethics, virtue and normative political action.

The process of managerial and leadership ethics relies upon personal responsibility, promise making and promise keeping. These depend upon self-awareness. People recognize and accept a position with its responsibilities, and doing justice to this position requires knowing oneself, monitoring the fit between person and position and adapting as the environment and position evolve under the pressures of political and organizational life. Individuals need to be aware of their values, responsibilities, strengths and limitations, especially as these are challenged and change within the demands of organizational life.

Self-awareness enables individuals to step back and assess their performance from deeper standards. At its best, it means people acquire self-awareness of their traits, learning and communicating styles. This awareness permits them to avoid being trapped by self-deception or an unyielding mindset. Understanding oneself means surfacing the diverse and lasting impacts of how a person is situated in a society and how deep-seated influences such as gender, ethnicity, race, class, geography or religion can influence what a person takes for granted, misses and buttresses their worldview and values with.

Good leaders understand their personal cognitive frames of judgment and with practice revise them in light of experience. They become aware of how they default to stereotypical portrayals of people and situations. This also enables them to avoid being trapped by their default frames into limited judgments. To know oneself is the groundwork of ethics and leading well.

Keeping self-awareness alive means attending to another critical theme in this book. A person needs to work hard to create and stay connected to a network of friends, peers and advisors. They can forge relationships where a person can get candid and caring feedback, criticism and support. This social space needs to exist beyond the work environment to create emotional and cognitive buffers to the normal human cognitive tendencies to become locked into groupthink or default understandings that may obscure ethical nuances or new challenges to individuals in the rush of daily life.

Managers need to be self-aware of how others rely upon their judgment and perceive their actions. Leaders are always on stage. They represent the authority and power of the institution and bridge the formal mission and aspirations with the gritty reality of task performance. Fellow managers, personnel, clients, activists and citizens watch leaders and look to managers and supervisors to model judgment and action. Self-awareness enables managers to be aware of mistakes, admit them and model learning and growth.

Self-awareness and personal integrity require the ability to pause and reflect, to stand back from the organizational inertia and pressure of a situation. Any decision environment under stress and time constraints will drive people to act quickly and default to existing frames of trained judgement and group understandings. This will be appropriate most of the time, but often enough, quickly defaulting to preferred cognitive frames misses critical new issues or overlooks new actors. Individuals can lock in prematurely to narrow understandings or scripts on issues. Cognitive frame lock, group think, heuristic confirmation bias or relying upon proximity or affiliation biases will all discourage individuals from active reflection to see the whole emerging situation. The cognitive and emotional discipline of being self-aware helps managers and leaders avoid these traps and expand the moral imagination of personal or group frames.

Bibliography

Applbaum, A. I. (1999). *Ethics for adversaries: The morality of roles in public and professional life*. Princeton, NJ: Princeton University Press.

Arendt, H. (1965). *Eichmann in Jerusalem: A report on the banality of evil*. New York, NY: Penguin.

Ashkenas, R. (2017, February 2). How to overcome executive isolation. *Harvard Business Review Newsletter*.

Badaracco, J. (1997). *Defining moments*. Cambridge, MA: Harvard Business School Press.

Badaracco, J. (2002). *Leading quietly: An unorthodox guide to doing the right thing*. Cambridge, MA: Harvard Business School Press.

Badaracco, J. (2016). Managing yourself: How to tackle your toughest decisions. *Harvard Business Review*, 104–107.

Bailey, S. K. (1964). Ethics and the public service. *Public Administration Review*, *24*(4), 234–243.

Bardach, E., & Kagan, R. A. (1982). *Going by the book: The problem of regulatory unreasonableness*. Philadelphia, PA: Temple University Press.

Bolman, L. G., & Deal, T. E. (2011). *Reframing organizations: Artistry, choice and leadership*. New York, NY: John Wiley & Sons.

Bowman, J. S. (Ed.). (1991). *Ethical frontiers in public management: Seeking new strategies to resolve ethical dilemmas*. San Francisco, CA: Jossey-Bass.

Bruce, W. (2001). *Classics of administrative ethics*. Boulder, CO. Westview Press.

Bryson, J., Crosby, B., & Bloomberg, L. (Ed.). (2015). *Creating public value in practice: Advancing the common good in a multi-sector, shared power, no-one-wholly-in-charge-world*. Boca Raton, FL: Taylor & Francis Group.

Burke, J. P. (1986). *Bureaucratic responsibility*. Baltimore, MD: The Johns Hopkins University Press.

Carter, S. L. (1996). *Integrity*. New York, NY: Basic Books.

Christensen, C. M., Allworth, J., & Dillon K. (2012). *How will you measure your life*? New York, NY: Harper Collins.

Ciulla, J. B. (2003). *The ethics of leadership*. Boston, MA: Wadsworth.

Cohen, S., & Eimicke, W. (2002). *The effective public manager: Achieving success in a changing government* (3rd edition). San Francisco, CA: Jossey-Bass.

Cooper, T. L. (1987). Hierarchy, virtue, and the practice of public administration: A perspective for normative ethics. *Public Administration Review*, *47*(4), 320–328.

Cooper, T. L. (2006). *The responsible administrator: An approach to ethics for the administrative role* (5th edition). San Francisco, CA: Jossey-Bass Publishers.

Cooper, T. L., & Wright, N. D. (Eds.). (1992). *Exemplary public administrators: Character and leadership in government*. San Francisco, CA: Jossey-Bass.

Crick, B. (1972). *In defence of politics* (2nd edition). Chicago, IL: University of Chicago Press.

Denhardt, K. G. (1988). *The ethics of public service*. New York, NY: Greenwood.

Dobel, J. P. (1990). *Compromise and political action: Political morality in liberal and democratic life*. Savage, MD: Rowman & Littlefield.

Dobel, J. P. (1990). Integrity in the public service. *Public Administration Review, 50*(3), 354–367.

Dobel, J. P. (1998). Political prudence and the ethics of leadership. *Public Administration Review, 58*(1), 74–81.

Dobel, J. P. (1999). *Public integrity*. Baltimore, MD: Johns Hopkins University Press.

Dobel, J. P. (2005). Managerial leadership and the ethical importance of legacy. *International Public Management Journal, 8*(2), 225–246.

Dobel, J. P. (2007). Public management as ethics. In Ferlie, E., Lynn, Jr., L. E., & Pollitt, C. (Eds.), *The Oxford handbook of public management* (pp. 156–181). Oxford, UK: Oxford University Press.

Doig, J. W. (1997). Leadership and innovation in the administrative state. *International Journal of Public administration, 20*(5), 861–879.

The European Ombudsman. (2003). *The European code for good administrative behavior*. Luxemburg: Office for Publications of the European Communities.

Fairhurst, G. T., & Sarr, R. A. (1996). *The art of framing: Managing the language of leadership*. San Francisco, CA: Jossey-Bass Publishers.

Farazmand, A. (1997). *Ethics, professionalism and the image of the public service: A report*. New York, NY: U.N. Secretariat.

Finer, H. (1941). Administrative responsibility in democratic government. *Public Administration Review, 1*(4), 335–350.

Frederickson, H. G. (1997). *The spirit of public administration*. San Francisco, CA: Jossey-Bass.

Frederickson, H. G., & Ghere, R. K. (Eds.). (2006). *Ethics in public management*. Armonk, NY: M. E. Sharpe.

Frederickson, H. G., & Ghere, R. K. (Eds.). (2013). *Ethics in public management* (2nd edition). Armonk, NY: M. E. Sharpe.

Gawande, A. (2010). *Checklist manifesto*. New York, NY: Penguin Books.

Geuras, D., & Garofalo, C. (2010). *Practical ethics in public administration*. Vienne, VA: Management Concepts Inc.

Goldhamer, H. (1978). *The advisor*. New York, NY: Elsevier.

Goodsell, C. (2011). *The mission mystique: Belief systems in public agencies*. Washington, DC: CQ Press.

Goodsell, C. (2015). *The new case for bureaucracy*. Washington, DC: CQ Press.

Gracian, B. (1993). *The art of worldly wisdom* (C. Maurer, Trans.). New York, NY: Doubleday.

Grant, A. M. (2013). *Give and take: A revolutionary approach to success*. New York, NY: Penguin.

Hampshire, S. (Ed.). (1978). *Public and private morality*. Cambridge, UK: Cambridge University Press.

Hart, D. K. (1974). Social equity, justice, and the equitable administrator. *Public Administration Review*, *34*(1), 3–11.

Hougaard, R., & Carter, J. (2017, December 19). If you aspire to be a great leader: Be present. *Harvard Business Review Newsletter*.

Huberts, L. (2014). *The integrity of governance: What it is, what we know, what is done and where to go*. Basingstoke, UK: Palgrave Macmillan.

Huberts, L., & Hoekstra, A. (Eds.). (2016). *Integrity management in the public sector: The Dutch approach* (pp. 146–158). The Hague: Bios.

Janis, I. L., & Mann, L. (1977). *Decision making: A psychological analysis of conflict, choice, and commitment*. New York, NY: Free Press.

Jurkiewicz, C. L. (2006). Power and ethics: The communal language of effective leadership. In Frederickson, G. H., & Ghere, R. K. (Eds.), *Ethics in public management* (pp. 95–113). Armonk, NY: M. E. Sharpe.

Kahneman, D. (2011). *Thinking, fast and slow*. New York, NY: Macmillan.

Kaplan, R. S., & Norton, D. P. (2004). *Strategy maps: Converting intangible assets into tangible outcomes*. Cambridge, MA: Harvard Business Press.

Kellerman, B. (2004). *Bad leadership: What it is, how it happens, why it matters*. Cambridge, MA: Harvard Business School Press.

Klein, G. A. (1998). *Sources of power: How people make decisions*. Cambridge, MA: MIT Press.

Klein, G. A. (2009). *Streetlights and shadows: Searching for the keys to adaptive decision making*. Cambridge, MA: MIT Press.

Korsgaard, C. M. (2009). *Self-constitution: Agency, identity and integrity*. Oxford, UK: Oxford University Press.

Kotter, J. P. (2001). *What leaders really do*. Cambridge, MA: Harvard Business School Publishing.

Kouzes, J. M., & Posner, B. Z. (2011). *Credibility: How leaders gain and lose it, why people demand it* (Vol. 244). New York, NY: John Wiley & Sons.

Lewis, C., & Gilman, S. C. (2005). *The ethics challenge in public service: A problem solving guide*. San Francisco, CA: Jossey-Bass.

Macaulay, M., & Lawton, A. (2006). From virtue to competence: Changing the principles of public service. *Public Administration Review*, *66*(5), 702–710.

Machiavelli, N. (1997). *The prince* (R. Adams, Trans. & Ed.). New York, NY: Norton Critical Editions.

Martin, R. C. (Ed.). (1965). *Public administration and democracy*. Syracuse, NY: Syracuse University Press.

Moore, M. M. (1995). *Creating public values: Strategic management in government*. Cambridge, MA: Harvard University Press.

O'Leary, R. (2006). *The ethics of dissent: Managing guerilla government*. Washington, DC: CQ Press.

O'Leary, R., & Bingham, L. B. (Eds.). (2009). *The collaborative public manager: New ideas for the twenty-first century*. Washington, DC: Georgetown University Press.

Price, T. (2008). *Leadership ethics: An introduction*. Cambridge, UK: Cambridge University Press.

Pritchard, M. S. (2006). *Professional integrity: Thinking ethically*. Lawrence, KS: University of Kansas Press.

Rainey, H. G. (2014). *Understanding and managing public organizations* (5th edition). San Francisco, CA: Jossey-Bass.

Rawls, J. (1971). *A theory of justice*. Cambridge, MA: Belknap Press of Harvard University Press.

Riordon, W. (1963). *Plunkitt of Tammany Hall*. New York, NY: Dutton.

Rohr, J. A. (1986). *To run a constitution: The legitimacy of the administrative state*. Lawrence, KS: University of Kansas Press.

Rohr, J. A. (1988). *Ethics for bureaucrats: An essay on law and values* (2nd edition). New York, NY: Marcel Dekker.

Rohr, J. A. (1999). *Public service, ethics and constitutional practice*. Lawrence, KS: University of Kansas Press.

Salomon, R. C. (1992). *Ethics and excellence: Co-operation and integrity in business*. Oxford, UK: Oxford University Press.

Schon, D. (1984). *The reflective practitioner: How professionals think in action*. New York, NY: Basic Books.

Selznick, P. (1957, 1984). *Leadership in administration: A sociological perspective*. New York, NY: Harper Collins.

Senge, P. M. (2006). *The fifth discipline: The art and practice of the learning organization*. New York, NY: Doubleday.

Svara, J. H. (2014). *The ethics primer for public administrators in government and nonprofit organizations*. Burlington, MA: Jones & Bartlett Publishers.

Terry, L. D. (2003). *Leadership of public bureaucracies: The administrator as conservator* (2nd edition). Armonk, NY: M. E. Sharpe.

Thompson, D. F. (1980). Moral responsibility in government: The problem of many hands. *American Political Science Review*, *74*, 905–916.

Thompson, D. F. (1987). *Political ethics and public office*. Cambridge, MA: Harvard University Press.

Thompson, D. F. (2005). *Restoring responsibility: Ethics in government, business, and healthcare* (Vol. 575). Cambridge, UK: Cambridge University Press.

Tudnem, R., & Burnes, B. (Eds.). (2013). *Organizational change, leadership, and ethics*. London, UK: Routledge.

Visser, H. (2016). Integrity incorporated in strategy and daily processes: The Netherlands Tax and Custom Administration. In Huberts, L., & Hoekstra, A. (Eds.), *Integrity management in the public sector: The Dutch approach* (pp. 146–158). The Hague: Bios.

Walzer, M. (1973). Political action: The problem of dirty hands. *Philosophy and Public Affairs*, *2*(2), 160–179.

Weber, M. (1958). Politics as a vocation. In Gerth, H. H. & Mills, W. W. (Ed. & Trans.), *From Max Weber: Essays in sociology* (pp. 77–128). Oxford, UK: Oxford University Press.

Williams, B. (1978). Politics and moral character. In Hampshire, S. (Ed.), *Public and private morality* (pp. 23–53). Cambridge, UK: Cambridge University Press.

Wilson, W. (1887). The study of administration. *Political Science Quarterly*, *2*(2), 197–222.

Zaleznik, A. (1992, 1977). Managers and leaders: Are they the same? *Harvard Business Review*, 126–135.

Zimbardo, P. (2007). *The Lucifer effect: Understanding how good people turn evil*. New York, NY: Random House.

3   Acting With Integrity

Individuals hold their values and beliefs together and make sense of their lives and actions through a sense of integrity. Integrity covers the entirety of a lived life. Seeking integrity in life helps individuals assert self-control and judgment when acting. Integrity flows from the process through which persons self-consciously articulate their beliefs, values and affiliations to themselves. They can then balance beliefs, values and affiliations to decide on the right action, and summon the courage and self-control to act upon those decisions.

Public Integrity

- The Nature of Integrity
- Public Integrity in Action—Domains of Judgment
- Personal Commitments and Capacities
- Obligations of Office
- Prudence and Effectiveness

The Nature of Integrity

Operationally individuals often express integrity through an ideal self or a hoped-for self that they set up as a powerful internal model to guide and assess their own behavior. This ideal self is often buttressed with strong social supports or affiliations. It can evolve and becomes a source of emotional motivation as well as disquiet when persons fail to live up to their ideal standards of conduct. Integrity is deeply implicated with self-awareness and responsibility. It depends upon the disciplined reflective capacity of a person to create cognitive and emotional distance from the situation before them, reflect upon it referring to an ideal self or standards of judgment and then guide action despite internal and external resistance to act.

This integrity approach to judgment resembles a process of weaving together the patterns of one's life into a whole self. Sometimes individuals may have to cut off or add sections to revise integrity and self in light of experiences of success or failure. Integrity may take on added responsibility with promises to add new domains to one's ideal self. Integrity resides in the stories individuals create to give consistency to their decisions. Integrity unfolds in mundane daily decisions that individuals constantly adjust to align with a sense of what is right or required by a position now linked to a sense of self by a promise. Sometimes, however, in situations of stress and temptation it requires individuals to pause, deliberate carefully, decide and act when sheer self-interest, temptation or unbridled emotion moves them in a different direction.

Public Integrity in Action—Domains of Judgment

Managerial leaders holding positions of official responsibility need to balance three domains of judgment as they decide and act. This triangulated set of relations grows from the moral structure of a person making a promise based upon their values and character and attending to the range of responsibilities inhering in an official position. Each is important and related to the others, and each should influence ethical decisions and actions. These are:

- Personal commitments and capacities
- Obligations of office
- Prudence and effectiveness

These three reference points do justice to the reality of the personal ethical self to give daily reality to the promises and obligations of a position. In addition, this range of decision domains underlines that managerial leaders are responsible for realistically attending to the organizational and policy realities of power and resources. Organizational solutions are not self-enforcing or self-sustaining. Organizational actions need the buttress of support over time or they become ineffective and meaningless. People are not given official responsibilities to be ineffective, and not attending to the power and resource dimensions of actions risks ethical negligence. This places prudence and effectiveness squarely in the ethical matrix for managers and leaders.

This model of public integrity provides an initial framework to organize managerial leaders' thinking. Faced with a challenge and opportunity to pause and reflect upon an issue, this cognitive framework helps the person to remember the source values and character that anchor their personal integrity and capacity to make and keep promises. These construct the psychological and ethical connections with the promise to abide by the authorizing standards of one's office or position. This connection and creative

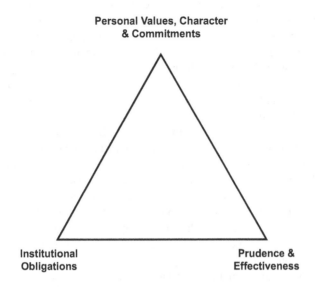

**Personal Values, Character
& Commitments**

**Institutional
Obligations**

**Prudence &
Effectiveness**

Diagram 3.1 Public Integrity: Domains of Judgment.

tension constitutes the motivation and direction of decisions and actions. The framework reminds public leaders that domains of adequate power and resources need to be built into all solutions and action. This framework provides the background frame for value driven leading that builds upon this basis to lay the integrity groundwork for the value driven leading model.

Managers and leaders unite these three domains together every time they make a decision. Leaders move from one to another as a check and clarification upon the requirements of action. Each area could be a viewed as a ray of light upon a subject that illuminates a different aspect of a situation. Each might be viewed as a different lens that clarifies a part of the moral terrain. As they overlap and reinforce each other, the ethical issues get more clear and detailed, and a leader's judgments become more complete and effective. The diagram above lays them out as a triangle where individuals can move from one point to another to guide and clarify action as they engage in the managerial task of building a value driven institution.

Personal Commitments and Capacities

This domain of judgment covers the values, skills and physical and character attributes individuals bring to an official position. These attributes are the basis for a leader's personal style and make each manager a unique leader. They exist prior to taking office and often bear on the reasons people are chosen, such as conscientiousness, prudence, energy, optimism, courage or trained professional judgment. Values and commitments may be grounded in family, profession and religion as well as the promise made when taking a position. One's ethnicity, gender, class or geography not only influences the person one is but often influences how a person is evaluated positively or negatively for a position. These aspects of self all serve as strengths and foundations, but they can also all serve as limitations on one's perception of people and situations.

A person's self-awareness permits them to become aware of the good and bad of these dimensions and work upon them, but above all, they must return to them in dialogue with the demands of a job or position. These multiple dimensions of selfhood have to be acknowledged and addressed even as they form the basis to express one's values and live one's character. Capacities flow from character but also from the physical and psychological attributes of a person. At their best, they reinforce each other, but it is entirely possible for personal commitments and capacities to conflict with the obligations of office.

This domain of personal character and values depends upon self-awareness and the capacity for self-mastery. In modern language, self-control and self-regulation means that a person can set intentions to achieve future goods and deploy internal psychological and external physical operations to achieve the desired end. This capacity for self-aware intention and focused psychological discipline buttresses the ability of a person to accept responsibility and accountability for decisions. The person devotes time, attention and energy to organize their life to develop the skills and resources to achieve the valued goals.

Obligations of Office

This domain of judgment flows from managers' conscientious fidelity to the institutional obligations of their positions. When individuals take on a position, they make a promise, implicit or explicit, to live up to the responsibilities of that position. A web of human beings and organizations rely upon a person's responsible and competent performance of their commitments. Superiors, colleagues, clients and citizens depend upon the competence and reliability of individuals who hold positions of power and authority.

In many organizations, individuals hold significant authority or power over vulnerable people like children, students or clients who need and depend upon people to perform their jobs well and with humanity. Whole classes of exposed citizens depend upon expert protection of the water and utilities or safety of food. Future or far away people depend upon attention to the quality of construction of projects or competent attention to public health, environmental or utilities policies. The obligations of equity and equal respect augment the normal organizational responsibilities and can be used to remind personnel about the enduring human impact of their "routine" jobs and responsibilities.

The duty to be transparent and accountable in actions can be as important as competence, reliability and inclusiveness. Ensuring reliable and true performance inheres not just in normal organizational hierarchy but also in the increasing need to attend to community deliberation to influence and above all assess the impact of organizations and policy. Both accountability and transparency place heavy obligations upon managerial leaders to ensure accurate and honest transference of information. This information permits honest evaluations of whether the actions are being performed, are competent and generating the consequences that the policy expects. Holding positions in this web of interdependency and vulnerability puts heavy burdens upon individuals to expend every effort to do their jobs well and in a competent manner with accountability.

Prudence and Effectiveness

This domain of judgment requires managers and leaders to attend to the context and power dimensions of their actions. Leaders more than anyone should understand the facts and the context of a situation before initiating action. Complications pervade the life of any organization. The environment is always evolving. Problems always arise or unanticipated consequences, opposition or questions emerge. For example, some individuals do not perform and others are good at some actions but limited; some clients pose dangers to themselves or maybe to staff. Other jobs may be understaffed or undertrained and slippage in performance occurs. Daily drudgework necessary to protect health and safety has to be done well and consistently to protect the welfare of everyone inside and outside the office. Technologies can alter dangers to health or the environment, create changes in the workplace or initiate new patterns of skill or accountability. Demographic changes can throw up new challenges or underserved populations.

The friction of dealing with powerful and resistant political actors can abrade the energy and competence of personnel at the point of task performance. This can be as simple as daily resistance to providing inspectors with good information or access, to using political influence with elected officials to put pressure upon senior managers of a service or regulatory agency. Yet individuals in official positions are not entrusted with public responsibilities to fail or let private power subvert task performance.

Managerial leaders who do not attend to developing their own resource, budget and power base to support their personnel in the field are ethically negligent. It takes power and courage, plus resources and budgets, to protect the core competence and performance of public purposes. Negligence, indifference or sloppy performance can ripple out with hidden but real adverse impacts upon human beings, often the adverse consequences are displaced to future citizens. It can be too easy to neglect or overlook people with less power and status denying them reasonable service or respect.

Implementing ethical and legal responsibilities requires managerial leaders to think about the proper means to achieve goals. They need to anticipate and prevent problems and know the context within which issues arise. Being prudent and addressing power involves identifying and connecting to the relevant actors who possess the resources but also the ability to prevent successful action. Prudent judgement involves anticipating challenges, adapting ethical and legal purposes to the constraints of organizational and political life and building durable projects to achieve the public goals.

Above all, prudence requires obtaining a thorough understanding of the different dimensions of a problem before acting. This type of knowledge requires learning about personnel, clients and conditions before problems arise and being able to respond professionally, not in rote, rigid or uninformed ways. Nor should people respond impulsively. Prudence requires individuals to not get stuck in their own cognitive framework or fall prey to their own confirmation biases but to understand other points of view and deploy multiple frameworks of understanding to address issues. If managers do not learn, listen and attend to the context, they risk being negligent and causing more problems. This poses a distinct obligation to uncover the facts and science of particular policy challenges. Finally, prudence involves the ability to be effective. This involves the capacity to map and deploy the sources of power and influence in an organization and to undertake concerted effort to build both capacity and support to sustain an organization's ability to perform its mission in difficult and shifting environments.

Attributes of Integrity-Based Action

- Accept Responsibility
- Act with Self-Control
- Reflect on Actions
- Seek Help and Support

Ethics depends upon a number of personal attributes that support the ability of persons to exercise self-awareness and keep integrity intact. These dimensions of personal, cognitive and emotional capacity support the very ability of a person to judge and act under pressure. Without them, people will not be able to consistently decide and act with a sustained commitment to values. They are critical for leaders to possess and instill in those they lead.

Personal integrity reinforces and makes possible organizational commitment to public purposes. A person's integrity is developed slowly through a self-conscious process of building habits that form frames of judgment that integrate emotions, cognitions, perceptions and physical actions. Ethical habits and durable integrity emerge from the engraved neural connections that reflective practice over time creates for individuals.

The habits permit fast and refined judgment under conditions demanding action and judgment. The habits emerge from frames and training and are linked to perception and identifying the situation and deploying action. It seems unconscious in its speed, but results from immense conscious reflection, practice and training. Educating oneself and others to engender habits is the essence of creating integrity and inculcating an ethical culture in an organization.

This accord of emotion and mind enables in a leader the judgment to discern with aptitude and quickness the significance of a situation and decide and act with alacrity. Perception is informed with intensity of emotional coding and intellectual recognition that swiftly identifies and motivates action. This activity reflects ethical commitment, practice, knowledge and candor in the person. Integrity enables a person to possess an intentionally created structure of disciplined perception and judgment that a person can deploy to pursue goals that the person regards as good. This structure is engraved through neural pathways and memory to be accessible for scanning the environment, judging and acting. These become the ongoing basis of professional judgment as a managerial leader.

Accept Responsibility

Self-mastery begins with the notion of possessing oneself. The human self with integrity comes down to the idea that a person has the ability to form an intention to guide actions. People can claim their purposes as their own and make promises upon them and execute upon the basis of the self-claimed purpose. The desired end enables the person to exercise internal discipline and focus to overcome internal and external obstacles and arrange attention, energy and time to act to further the intent. Responsible and trained persons seeking goals can repress, set aside or channel internal emotions and demands that resist their purpose.

This aligns the earlier importance of self-awareness with integrity and promise making with taking responsibility for a position and actions. The idea of being responsible places the obligation to learn the skills and understand the context squarely upon the individual actor. A responsible actor takes on the obligation to focus attention, energy and time to learn the skills required to achieve a goal, and also the more complicated commitment to self-correction. Others cannot make a person better, but they can help; individuals must undertake this.

Being responsible gives action more ethical value. Being responsible imposes an obligation to be "fully present" to all aspects of situation. This presence involves bringing the full array of one's skills and energy to a task. It also opens the person to the full range of situational awareness and the need to learn. Being present and open increases the chances that a person will not let the past dominate decisions and actions when challenges arise. Being present resists unreflectively following a particular interpretation of the rules.

People know and acknowledge the legal and moral obligations that come with a position. Accepting responsibility increases a person's commitment to act competently. It minimizes the blame game and the temptation to shirk giving full time and commitment to achieve goals.

Act With Self-Control

The ability to control emotions and impulses is fundamental to effective managing and leading. A leader or manager with integrity must possess self-mastery that integrates the emotional, cognitive and perceptual aspects of selfhood. This builds on personal responsibility, where persons take control of internal actions to align cognitive capacity to master ideals, rules and goals. This demands study and practice to constantly learn and master form and technique. This type of self-disciplined learning requires truthfulness and adaptation.

Self-control enables leaders to live up to promises despite temptations, obstacles and attempts to manipulate them. Self-control enables managerial leaders to bring their attention to bear on critical issues and act on priorities under stress. Self-control helps managers live at the intersection of major challenges where they are the front line of institutional responsibility.

Managers should control their emotions and especially their temper as well as likes and dislikes. If personnel and those served by an agency believe a manager or supervisor "loses it" easily, they will act in ways that manipulate and control a quick-tempered or impetuous manager. If managers cannot control their prejudices, they will underutilize the possibilities of diversity, precipitate tensions and leave the institution open to lawsuits. Their impulsive actions will undermine the legitimacy of other leaders in the agency and generate uncertainty within the culture about expectations and norms. Not controlling likes and dislikes makes people vulnerable to charges of favoritism that will undermine trust and credibility. Self-control or self-mastery is a foundation of ethical and professional behavior.

Reflect on Actions

Gut instincts are not good enough. Instinct, while occasionally right, often carries the weight of years of socialized and thoughtless prejudices or past habits that may be inappropriate for present conditions. Gut reactions flow from internalized frames of reference that may or may not be appropriate to a particular situation.

Experienced managerial leaders have developed through practicing and learning trained intuitions. Most daily judgments flow from this matrix of trained intuition and engaged reality. But the flow of reality always creates surprises and unexpected problems; defaulting to even trained frames can miss nuances of a challenge.

Good ethical leading requires the ability to pause and stand back from personal and organizational default frames of reference. Good leaders access different frames of reference to understand all the dimensions of a situation, especially in times of change and stress. Ethics and prudence require thoughtful consideration of the obligations, laws, rules and stakes in a situation, as well as an assessment of the consequences before acting. In a world of partners and collaboration, leaders need to understand and connect with the differing organizational beliefs, interests and missions of relevant actors. Without this careful awareness of complexity and multiple relationships, building partnerships and collaborations will falter.

Reflective practice can build up strong moral intuitions supported by internalized frameworks, but even trained intuitions can become thoughtless default frames of judgment. They need to be tested regularly in dialogue with diverse others such as team members, partners or communities. Managers balance several different obligations and must be aware of them all. Managerial leaders in public and nonprofit organizations possess a strong obligation to know the laws and rules, but also the context and people in a situation. Managerial leaders model behavior for colleagues, subordinates, collaborators, clients and citizens. Every action sets a precedent, shapes expectations and influences how people will behave in the future.

Seek Help and Support

No one can do it alone. Keeping one's integrity viable, especially when exercising responsibility in organizations, depends upon ensuring that individuals have relationships outside of the immediate organizational setting to get ethical and emotional distance from the pressures of authority. One of the regular traps of leadership is to become isolated from personnel or face distorted reports from subordinates. Managerial leaders have to work constantly to ensure that they have places where people can candidly discuss the issues that challenge and vex leaders outside of the immediate circle of power and interests.

Friends, respected colleagues and superiors can help reveal the full range of ethical issues and obligations in a particular situation. Peers outside of the chain of command understand the full range of pressures one faces and can provide support and insight that people can lose in the stress of work. Such personal allies can help people see themselves with greater accuracy and can challenge default reactions, groupthink and personal inconsistency; assess unanticipated consequences; and forge better decisions. Relying upon trusted professional colleagues and friends or external networks of support helps sustain not only accurate self-reflection but also the emotional and psychological endurance needed to bring energy and commitment to the position.

Threats to Integrity

- Isolation and Distortion
- Denial of Responsibility
- Rigidity
- Peer Culture
- Dominant Informal Actors
- Diversity Challenges
- Silence

Individual integrity anchors the capacity of managers and leaders to implement the mission of the organization. Personal integrity supports a commitment to the mission values, the space for reflection on them and the strength to implement them over time when adapting to changing conditions. Integrity provides the psychological strength to keep moving while facing the daily friction of opposition and resource limitations. Shared values and commitments provide a robust depth to an organization's ability to address the myriad external pressures to undermine or coopt their tasks and missions.

Integrity depends upon the capacity for taking personal responsibility. Integrity-based responsibility shores up the value- and culture-based decisions and provides an antidote to postulating all organizations as self-interested coalitions activated and fraught with tensions between principals and agents or selfishness and broader aims. It provides the model to think of organizations and people as possessing the capacity for institutional role commitments. With this capacity, personnel can make and implement decisions guided by broader committed values beyond self-interest supported by colleagues.

Given the importance of integrity, responsibility and culture, maintaining individual and organizational integrity is an ongoing leadership task. Yet myriad internal and external pressures that press upon an organization's people and can erode their values and missions. Anticipating these stresses and addressing them in oneself and in the organization are critical aspects of active leadership. These pressures can include:

*   Daily friction of interpersonal relations
*   Daily friction associated with diverse professional and personal identities
*   Pressure to meet impossible goals
*   Sense of being unacknowledged and underpaid
*   Protective subcultures within a larger culture
*   Seeking to escape unreasonable oversight or maximize autonomy
*   Outsiders seeking to capture or influence an organization for their purposes
*   Individuals trying to coopt or wear down personnel to achieve their personal goals
*   Competitors seeking resources
*   Indifference or hypocrisy of senior managers

These cumulative daily stresses can drive individuals and groups to adapt social, psychological and ethical stances that reduce the physical and psychological stress of being underappreciated, under resourced or pressed to subvert their jobs by insiders and outsiders. The cognitive, emotional and ethical strategies to reduce stress and come to terms with underperforming or distorted goals can lead to self-deception. People revise their own sense of ideal self or live in denial of what they are now failing to achieve. This denial and self-deception can settle into a group-supported, stable belief system even if it exists at a suboptimal level of performance or ethics. These approaches can be contagious to other personnel. They can hide adverse ethical consequences or responsibilities for indifferent or corrupt performance.

This section details predictable forces and psychological and ethical patterns that individuals experience facing the pressure and dysfunction of organizational life. Being self-aware of these dangers permits leaders to pay attention to themselves and personnel in order to anticipate and combat such traps for integrity and performance.

Isolation and Distortion

All persons in a position of authority face persistent attrition of their integrity. This attrition affects their decision making from a distortion field of power and position around them. Even small increments of power and authority can give persons control over another person's career paths, rewards and daily quality of life. This power/position equation leads people around managerial leaders to be careful in the information they convey. No one wants to convey brutal facts, raw data or bad news to let persons know they are failing in their leading. The distortion fields do not so much encourage outright dishonesty as holding back information or repacking it in ways to soften or hide the impact. People worry about what a leader wants to hear or what they believe a manager wants to hear and craft their information accordingly. No one wants to arouse ire or bad will for conveying bad news.

This form of distortion isolates managerial leaders from what is going on around them or on the line. It creates a good news cocoon and does not provide adequate warning when things are going badly. Without self-conscious efforts to address its effects, this distortion field makes it very difficult for managerial leaders to access the weak signals or emerging data that point to slippages in performance, looming shifts in the environment or internal pressures that undermine performance.

This distortion of information and isolation from bad news or weak signals of future challenges can be amplified since manager's attention is diffused by an inundation of mundane problems and decisions. It gets worse as people move up the hierarchy. They are expected to speak, decide and direct action. These expectations for decisiveness can undermine a leader's discipline to wait, listen and elicit needed information from reluctant subordinates or colleagues. This information is critical when addressing emerging problems and long-term opportunities.

Denial of Responsibility

Making decisions and taking responsibility for the quality and consequences of personal actions provides immense long-term satisfaction and strength to individuals. It reinforces integrity and character and models how personnel can embrace decision and adapt to action. The reality, however, of making decisions that impact the world and people can cause anxiety and agitation for many individuals. In addition, many organizations assess, reward or promote on the basis of perceived consequences of action. As a result of these psychological costs and professional stakes, many people demure or avoid responsibility for taking actions with which they are charged.

Individuals can avoid a difficult decision or avoid the painful consequences of actions through a denial of responsibility. Denial permits individuals to decide or act, but to ultimately blame the problem on others. "I was only following orders" has justified horrible violations of human welfare and abuses of power. Individuals have been denying responsibility since bureaucracy was invented by stating they were are following "the letter of the law" or acting on incomplete information. The excuses are endless.

They all enable action but deflect responsibility to some other person, entity or external condition.

The denial of responsibility tempts all managers because the jobs are complicated and taxing, the consequences difficult and decisions fraught with ambiguity. Often managers may need to discipline fellow employees or draw lines around behavior that will make them unpopular. Moreover, managers may receive harmful, stupid or questionable directives, yet feel an obligation to follow them. The world of modern governance with its multiple partnerships and dispersed authority and accountability makes it even more difficult to isolate clear responsibility. This confusion of the chain of command creates an ethical space for possible innovation but often paralyzes individuals or creates drift and inertia with no responsibility to anyone.

Rigidity

A variation on the denial of responsibility lies in rigidly following orders, or "going by the book." This response protects people from second-guessing and is a great "cover your ass" tactic. Rigid, by-the-book tactics pretend that people have scant choices with a well-understood situation and no potential complications. This excuse assumes that the existing rules are clear, information complete and the consequences of applying the rules are easily apparent. Such situations rarely ever arise. Nonetheless, a rigid approach reassures individuals, removes responsibility for taking the initiative and minimizes stress in the job. It also protects the deciders from second-guessing, even if the actions are inappropriate or the situation results in easily foreseen bad consequences. It reduces people to machines with no discretion or judgment. It also means managers or supervisors are not motivated to learn the context or nuances of situations and people.

Peer Culture

The real norms of action are carried by the values that people use to guide their daily actions outside of direct oversight by senior managers. Groups develop operationalized ethics through their cultures, which involve internalized peer norms of perception and judgement. People are socialized into these norms by constant interaction with colleagues who affirm them and punish deviance in many nuanced ways. Peer groups carry and sustain the daily professional judgments of individuals in organizations.

Subtle and not so subtle peer pressures push individuals to act in certain ways. Regardless of the high-sounding values of the mission, groups of individuals who are just trying to get by or meet impossible goals often develop their own cultures that have little relation to the values espoused at the top. Groups of people face a lack of resources, constant pressure from outside and unrealistic quotas for action, and they must figure out ways to adapt to these incessant pressures. Often, they feel unsupported and under-managed, so dangerous, illegal or unethical behavior can become embedded in peer culture. People who try to change it can be endangered by peers or retaliated against for violating group norms or snitching on them. One of the primary obligations of managers and supervisors is to work to understand and influence the peer culture of groups within an institution.

Dominant Informal Actors

All informal cultures, especially in relatively small units, are vulnerable to the excessive influence of single individuals. Sometimes it might be an experienced "old pro" or an "expert" whom everyone needs or who provides favors. Often individuals acquire "indispensable" expertise or create networks of reliance upon them. This reliance makes them almost invulnerable to direct administrative accountability. Often times they control vital resources of budget and parse out these resources based on favoritism. Individual personnel, clients or served citizens may gravitate to them for advice and support, sometimes at odds with the formal rules of the organization or the manager. Identifying these actors, limiting or controlling them, co-opting or winning them over is critical to influence informal culture and norms. In a world dependent upon partnerships with high turnover among actors, such privileged personnel also thrive with informal control of resources, knowledge or networks and can deflect the purpose of partnerships and resources for their own private ends.

The most dangerous case arises when an individual uses coercion and fear to control others. Bullies exist in all organizations, and organizations where inequality in power exists, or where clients are more vulnerable or less educated, are susceptible to such individuals. The bullying can be as simple as allocating one's time or resources based on favoritism or holding back support to punish people who do not do one's bidding. The bullies take advantage of emotional control and their own network to ostracize others. These networks can protect abuse of clients, resources or fellow personnel out of a combination of fear and affiliation. Most informal work cultures have a code of silence that reinforces the potential power of resource controlling, violent, abusive or uncontrolled bullies. Managers can lose control of their areas to such individuals and destroy the capacity of their unit to perform well or behave ethically or legally. Engaging such informal actors and bullies is slow, bitter work and takes time, energy and political capital; it can be exhausting, but it is vital to recapture and build a culture of integrity and competence.

Diversity Challenges

Effective leading of modern organizations requires integrating a wide array of professional, organizational and diverse people into cohering teams. Managing complex partnerships as well as getting the best decisions builds heavily upon integrating diverse groups and points of view into sound decision making and sustained implementation.

Government and nonprofit organizations serve diverse populations and often address deep structural inequalities or boundaries where unequal actors come into contact. The reality of legal, social and economic inequalities creates a system where many users or potential users of key public and nonprofit services such as welfare, schools, corrections or health care are racial and ethnic minorities. In addition, many of the most vulnerable rely heavily upon public utilities, public health and environmental regulations as outsider populations. Often these served populations differ from the staff population along ethnic, racial, religious and gender lines.

This reality can produce systematic mistreatment or underservice for structurally unequal groups. This reality can produce a tinderbox where small sparks of perceived disrespect can flame into anger, misunderstanding or violence. The reality can also lead to cumulative implicit bias in the performance of jobs over time when the different populations encounter each other. Often these incidents precipitate legal struggles. The same divisions can carry over into organizational life. People possess well-documented tendencies to affiliate with people who are like them, whether they be professional affiliation, religion, race, gender or many myriad variations of human differentiation. This can lead to isolation and subcultures within an organization where insulated units, groups or cliques generate loyalty to groups that can conflict with the commitment to the organization's common mission. These tensions pervade and overlay everyday life and can erode trust and relations among personnel, leaders and citizens. Managerial leaders committed to building a culture of integrity and mission-based performance have to attend to differences. They should devote special attention to the boundaries where structural inequality undermines quality of service.

Silence

Modern history and psychology reinforce a reality for human beings—people who know they are protected by secrecy or silence will often perform immoral actions that they never would do if they knew they would be held publicly accountable for them. Cultures of silence make possible levels of abuse of power that can endanger justice and the rights and safety of personnel or clients. Hidden actions against the vulnerable, whether they be dementia patients in a nursing home or mentally ill homeless people, can become imbedded in a subculture and go unreported by fellow workers.

People will look the other way in the name of solidarity with fellow workers. Silence muffles accountability and reporting that are the lifeblood of learning and reform. Silence hides actions, permits forbidden actions and undercuts real accountability. Silence can become a solace and stance for individuals who were once committed but are discouraged, burnt-out or cynical. It is the ally of pathological peer culture, dominant individuals or deep discrimination and abuse. Attending to the temptations to silence and the natural inclination of groups to protect their members is a never-ending demand of managerial leading.

Bibliography

Adams, G. B., & Balfour, D. L. (2009). *Unmasking administrative evil* (3rd edition). Armonk, NY: M. E. Sharpe.

Applbaum, A. I. (1999). *Ethics for adversaries: The morality of roles in public and professional life*. Princeton, NJ: Princeton University Press.

Arendt, H. (1965). *Eichmann in Jerusalem: A report on the banality of evil*. New York, NY: Penguin.

Ashkenas, R. (2017, February 2). How to overcome executive isolation. *Harvard Business Review Newsletter*.

Badaracco, J. (1997). *Defining moments*. Cambridge, MA: Harvard Business School Press.

Badaracco, J. (2002). *Leading quietly: An unorthodox guide to doing the right thing*. Cambridge, MA: Harvard Business Press.

Badaracco, J. (2016). Managing yourself: How to tackle your toughest decisions. *Harvard Business Review*, 104–107.

Bailey, S. K. (1964). Ethics and the public service. *Public Administration Review*, *24*(4), 234–243.

Bazerman, M. H., & Tenbrunsel, A. E. (2011). *Blind spots: Why we fail to do what's right and what to do about it*. Princeton, NJ: Princeton University Press.

Bolman, L. G., & Deal, T. E. (2011). *Reframing organizations: Artistry, choice and leadership*. New York, NY: John Wiley & Sons.

Bowman, J. S. (Ed.). (1991). *Ethical frontiers in public management: Seeking new strategies to resolve ethical dilemmas*. San Francisco, CA: Jossey-Bass.

Bruce, W. (2001). *Classics of administrative ethics*. Boulder, CO: Westview Press.

Bryson, J., Crosby, B., & Bloomberg, L. (Eds.). (2015). *Creating public value in practice: Advancing the common good in a multi-sector, shared power, no-one-wholly-in-charge-world*. Boca Raton, FL: Taylor & Francis Group.

Burke, J. P. (1986). *Bureaucratic responsibility*. Baltimore, MD: The Johns Hopkins University Press.

Carter, S. L. (1996). *Integrity*. New York, NY: Basic Books.

Christensen, C. M., Allworth, J., & Dillon, K. (2012). *How will you measure your life?* New York, NY: Harper Collins.

Ciulla, J. B. (2003). *The ethics of leadership.* Boston, MA: Wadsworth.

Cooper, T. L. (1987). Hierarchy, virtue, and the practice of public administration: A perspective for normative ethics. *Public Administration Review, 47*(4), 320–328.

Cooper, T. L. (2006). *The responsible administrator: An approach to ethics for the administrative role* (5th edition). San Francisco, CA: Jossey-Bass Publishers.

Cooper, T. L., & Wright, N. D. (Eds.). (1992). *Exemplary public administrators: Character and leadership in government.* San Francisco, CA: Jossey-Bass.

Denhardt, K. G. (1988). *The ethics of public service.* New York, NY: Greenwood.

Dobel, J. P. (1990). *Compromise and political action: Political morality in liberal and democratic life.* Savage, MD: Rowman & Littlefield.

Dobel, J. P. (1990). Integrity in the public service. *Public Administration Review, 50*(3), 354–367.

Dobel, J. P. (1998). Political prudence and the ethics of leadership. *Public Administration Review, 58*(1), 74–81.

Dobel, J. P. (1999). *Public integrity.* Baltimore, MD: Johns Hopkins University Press.

Dobel, J. P. (2005). Managerial leadership and the ethical importance of legacy. *International Public Management Journal, 8*(2), 225–246.

Dobel, J. P. (2007). Public management as ethics. In Ferlie, E., Lynn, Jr., L. E., & Pollitt, C. (Eds.), *The Oxford handbook of public management* (pp. 156–181). Oxford, UK: Oxford University Press.

Dobel, J. P. (2015). What athletic achievement can teach about ethics. *Public Integrity, 17*(4), 319–330.

The European Ombudsman. (2003). *The European code for good administrative behavior.* Luxemburg: Office for Publications of the European Communities.

Fairhurst, G. T., & Sarr, R. A. (1996). *The art of framing: Managing the language of leadership.* San Francisco, CA: Jossey-Bass Publishers.

Farazmand, A. (1997). *Ethics, professionalism and the image of the public service: A report.* New York, NY: U.N. Secretariat.

Finer, H. (1941). Administrative responsibility in democratic government. *Public Administration Review, 1*(4), 335–350.

Fleishman, J. et al. (1981). *Public duties: The moral obligations of government officials.* Cambridge, MA: Harvard University Press.

Frederickson, H. G. (1997). *The spirit of public administration.* San Francisco, CA: Jossey-Bass.

Frederickson, H. G., & Ghere, R. K. (Eds.). (2006). *Ethics in public management.* Armonk, NY: M. E. Sharpe.

Frederickson, H. G., & Ghere, R. K. (Eds.). (2013). *Ethics in public management* (2nd edition). Armonk, NY: M. E. Sharpe.

Goodsell, C. (2011). *The mission mystique: Belief systems in public agencies.* Washington, DC: CQ Press.

Gracian, B. (1993). *The art of worldly wisdom* (C. Maurer, Trans.). New York, NY: Doubleday.

Hampshire, S. (Ed.). (1978). *Public and private morality*. Cambridge, UK: Cambridge University Press.

Hougaard, R., & Carter, J. (2017, December 19). If you aspire to be a great leader: Be present. *Harvard Business Review Newsletter*.

Huberts, L. (2014). *The integrity of governance: What it is, what we know, what is done and where to go*. Basingstoke, UK: Palgrave Macmillan.

Jackall, R. (1988). *Moral mazes: The world of corporate managers*. Oxford, UK: Oxford University Press.

Janis, I. L. (1982). *Groupthink: Psychological studies of policy decisions and fiascoes*. Boston, MA: Houghton Mifflin.

Janis, I. L., & Mann, L. (1977). *Decision making: A psychological analysis of conflict, choice, and commitment*. New York, NY: Free Press.

Johnson, R. A. (2003). *Whistleblowing: When it works—and why*. Boulder, CO: L. Rienner Publishers.

Jurkiewicz, C. L. (Ed.). (2015). *The foundations of organizational evil*. London, UK: Routledge.

Kahneman, D. (2011). *Thinking, fast and slow*. New York, NY: Macmillan.

Kaplan, R. S., & Norton, D. P. (2004). *Strategy maps: Converting intangible assets into tangible outcomes*. Cambridge, MA: Harvard Business Press.

Klein, G. A. (1998). *Sources of power: How people make decisions*. Cambridge, MA: MIT Press.

Klein, G. A. (2009). *Streetlights and shadows: Searching for the keys to adaptive decision making*. Cambridge, MA: MIT Press.

Korsgaard, C. M. (2009). *Self-constitution: Agency, identity and integrity*. Oxford, UK: Oxford University Press.

Kouzes, J. M., & Posner, B. Z. (2006). *The leadership challenge* (Vol. 3). New York, NY: John Wiley & Sons.

Kouzes, J. M., & Posner, B. Z. (2011). *Credibility: How leaders gain and lose it, why people demand it* (Vol. 244). New York, NY: John Wiley & Sons.

Lewis, C., & Gilman, S. C. (2005). *The ethics challenge in public service: A problem solving guide*. San Francisco, CA: Jossey-Bass.

Macaulay, M., & Lawton, A. (2006). From virtue to competence: Changing the principles of public service. *Public Administration Review, 66*(5), 702–710.

Machiavelli, N. (1997). *The prince* (R. Adams, Trans. & Ed.). New York, NY: Norton Critical Editions.

March, J. G., & Olsen, J. P. (2010). *Rediscovering institutions*. New York, NY: Simon and Schuster.

Milgrim, S. (1975). *Obedience to authority*. New York: Harper Torchbooks.

Moberg, D. J. (2000). Role models and moral exemplars: How do employees acquire virtues by observing others? *Business Ethics Quarterly, 10*(3), 675–696.

Moberg, D. J. (2006). Ethics blind spots in organizations: How systematic errors in person perception undermine moral agency. *Organization Studies, 27*(3), 413–428.

Moore, M. M. (1995). *Creating public values: Strategic management in government*. Cambridge, MA: Harvard University Press.

Nagel, T. (1978). Ruthlessness in public life. In Hampshire, S. (Ed.), *Public and private morality* (pp. 75–92). Cambridge, UK: Cambridge University Press.

O'Leary, R., & Bingham, L. B. (Eds.). (2009). *The collaborative public manager: New ideas for the twenty-first century.* Washington, DC: Georgetown University Press.

O'Leary, R. (2006). *The ethics of dissent: Managing guerilla government.* Washington, DC: CQ Press.

OECD. (1998). *Principles for managing government ethics.* PUMA Policy Brief. Retrieved May 12, 2017 from: www.oecd.org/puma/gvrnance/ethics/index/htm

OECD. (2000). *Trust in government: Ethics measures in OECD countries.* Paris: OECD.

Price, T. (2008). *Leadership ethics: An introduction.* Cambridge, UK: Cambridge University Press.

Pritchard, M. S. (2006). *Professional integrity: Thinking ethically.* Lawrence, KS: University of Kansas Press.

Rawls, J. (1971). *A theory of justice.* Cambridge, MA: Belknap Press of Harvard University Press.

Rohr, J. A. (1986). *To run a constitution: The legitimacy of the administrative state.* Lawrence, KS: University of Kansas Press.

Rohr, J. A. (1988). *Ethics for bureaucrats: An essay on law and values* (2nd edition). New York, NY: Marcel Dekker.

Rohr, J. A. (1999). *Public service, ethics and constitutional practice.* Lawrence, KS: University of Kansas Press.

Sabato, L. J. (1991). *Feeding frenzy: Attack journalism in American politics.* New York, NY: The Free Press.

Salomon, R. C. (1992). *Ethics and excellence: Co-operation and integrity in business.* Oxford, UK: Oxford University Press.

Schon, D. (1984). *The reflective practitioner: How professionals think in action.* New York, NY: Basic Books.

Selznick, P. (1957, 1984). *Leadership in administration: A sociological perspective.* New York, NY: Harper Collins.

Senge, P. M. (2006). *The fifth discipline: The art and practice of the learning organization.* New York, NY: Doubleday.

Terry, L. D. (2003). *Leadership of public bureaucracies: The administrator as conservator* (2nd edition). Armonk, NY: M. E. Sharpe.

Thompson, D. F. (1980). Moral responsibility in government: The problem of many hands. *American Political Science Review, 74,* 905–916.

Thompson, D. F. (1987). *Political ethics and public office.* Cambridge, MA: Harvard University Press.

Thompson, D. F. (2005). *Restoring responsibility: Ethics in government, business, and healthcare* (Vol. 575). Cambridge, UK: Cambridge University Press.

Uhr, J. (2015). *Prudential public leadership: Promoting ethics in public policy and administration.* Basingstoke, UK: Palgrave MacMillan.

Walzer, M. (1973). Political action: The problem of dirty hands. *Philosophy and Public Affairs, 2*(2), 160–179.

Weber, M. (1958). Politics as a vocation. In Gerth, H. H., & Mills, W. W. (Ed. & Trans.), *From Max Weber: Essays in sociology* (pp. 77–128). Oxford, UK: Oxford University Press.

Williams, B. (1978). Politics and moral character. In Hampshire, S. (Ed.), *Public and private morality* (pp. 23–53). Cambridge, UK: Cambridge University Press.

Wilson, W. (1887). The study of administration. *Political Science Quarterly, 2*(2), 197–222.

Zimbardo, P. (2007). *The Lucifer effect: Understanding how good people turn evil.* New York, NY: Random House.

4 Building an Ethical Organization

The political and social environment of public and nonprofit organizations generates endless pressures that can undermine the integrity of managers and supervisors. The same pressures abrade performance at the point of task performance and slowly erode high performance standards. Systematic structural attention and incentive and accountability programs are vital to address these endless currents. However, the key to counter these forces at the daily decision level lies in creating an ethical performance culture.

Managerial leaders need to focus constantly upon the mission of the organization and ensure that the persons working on a task connect the mission with their personal promise with their daily competence and impact upon the world. To achieve this, managerial leaders need to attune their self-awareness and attention to ensuring people at the point of task performance have support for critical knowledge, trust, respect and independent judgment. Managerial leaders need the ability to see a situation in the entire context; model appropriate behavior and values; educate employees on an ongoing basis; enforce the boundaries of behavior; and seek help and support when necessary.

Committed organizational leaders strive to integrate the values of the person with the values of the mission and work to ensure that these values and character infuse task performance. Managerial leaders need to amass the power and support to influence and counteract environmental pressures as well to support and protect individuals committed to the mission. They need to use power and support to combat internal resistance to promoting the values and performance required by the mission.

The challenge presents itself as another strategic triangle for internal management where leaders iterate and align across the commitments of the individual to the mission and organizational purpose. They need to work to infuse meaning into the competence and judgments of people in daily task performance. Jobs and positions are then sustained by commitment not just compliance. This approach highlights several strategic focal points

Diagram 4.1 Mission/Person/Task Alignment

that managerial leaders should work to master. They need to focus upon the management triangle that aligns the mission–person–task to provide support and meaning for personnel.

Focal Points of Ethical Management

- Cultivate Organizational Purpose
- Know the Purpose of the Rules and Laws
- Build Trust, Respect and Communication
- Embrace Discretion
- Protect the Core
- Engage the Whole Context
- Model and Educate
- Exercise Courage and Endurance
- Seek Help and Support

Cultivate Organizational Purpose

Vision, mission, goals and outcomes all embody the deeper leadership and management task of cultivating an abiding sense of purpose for the organization, groups and persons. The modern disconnect between meaning and work extracts huge performance costs in organizations and makes individuals more vulnerable to minimum competence, indifference or thoughtless abuse of position. Purpose reveals itself as the intent that guides people performing tasks. Values and commitments manifest themselves in purpose; purpose provides moral intent and motivation underneath commitments. It can fill in the emotional and cognitive gaps when rules face reality. Having a sense of purpose offsets the casual and slow erosion of belief in the competence and importance of one's job. If leaders can help groups imbue daily tasks with intention, meaning and direction, they can increase the quality of human dignity and performance in the organization. Nurturing purpose in persons and relations creates the deep structure that supports organizational culture, mission, decisions and goals.

Know the Purpose of Rules and Laws

All aspects of organizational integrity depend upon managers and supervisors knowing the mission, laws, codes and rules that guide their work. They need to understand not just the letter of the rules, but the purposes behind regulations and procedures. The laws and processes give reality to the purposes of a group or organization. They are put in place to achieve levels of consistency of performance and accountability to authorizers. Often, they reflect the best practice in light of professional and scientific knowledge, or they emerge from complex political negotiations. In addition, the rules and standards possess effective input into what professional excellence looks like, or how to attend to safety and welfare issues for people and personnel. Mastering this knowledge gives managers the ability to understand the foundations of competence. It informs their discretion and permits them to exercise it when rigid enforcement of rules is inappropriate or dangerous.

Government and nonprofit work involves high levels of professional expertise to address the demands of the common good such as public safety, health, social services or environmental or public utility charges. The expertise involved in these complex professions are often enshrined in professional codes of ethics. These codes clarify standards of competence and values to fill in the spaces of the rules. Many situations require that officials bring to bear professional knowledge and standards such as those involved in engineering, public health, medicine, corrections, law and many areas of organizational life. This professional knowledge lays down powerful baselines of competence and often provides clear minimum standards of safety or competence. They can serve as checklists to inform deliberation around decisions. Understanding and supporting these standards is a critical aspect of knowledge and accountability.

At the same time, the professional knowledge needs to be complemented by awareness of how expertise and regulations may not fully grasp the complex reality on the ground. One of the common misunderstandings arises when professionals do not understand the cultural and ethnic background of communities. Their own "professional" judgments may not account for how these will be perceived by different communities. In addition, the professionals and organizations may lack insight into significant nuances that need to be addressed with engaging communities with different identities or cultural assumptions. It also arises when facing obdurate opposition based upon economic self-interest that seeks to wear down professional will or exhaust the resources of an agency through litigation or political back filling. Long-term and successful impacts depend upon developing context informed professional expertise that leaders need to work for. Managers and supervisors have strong legal and ethical obligations to master the knowledge of law and rules and gain the competence needed to do their jobs; otherwise they will be negligent, ineffective and possibly dangerous to the health of their organizations.

Build Trust, Respect and Communication

- *Trust:* Successful leading at all levels depends upon building trust with workers, colleagues, clients and outside groups. Trust depends upon mutual reliability of expectations for each other as well as the ability to rely upon a person's promise or performance. In a world of partnerships and collaboration, creating institutional trust is even more vital to bring alignment and learning across the cooperating bodies. Without trust people's compliance will be lower, secrecy will be higher, defaults higher and enforcement costs will grow because once the manager or supervisor is gone from the scene, individuals will revert to their preferred informal patterns of behavior. Outsiders will take advantage of this break in the culture and norms to try to influence or get special treatment. On the other hand, respect and trust are created carefully over time, but can be lost very quickly.

  Trust creates resilience across members of the organization and increases the efficiency of communication and coordination. The foundation of organizational trust lies in consistency in promise keeping and performance. How a leader is trusted will build further upon a leader's sustained competence, fairness and respectful actions.

  These consistent actions build a belief in people that a leader has their back and frees workers to act with integrity and competence, believing that management will support them when they face opposition or subversion. Without competence, fairness or respect, people will lack trust for leadership. This leads to resisting or ignoring leaders. Workers will ignore directives, take matters into their own hands or use silence and peer groups to hide suboptimal performance. Trust creates social capital and resources to help groups endure external and internal challenges, maintain cohesion and adapt to new challenges.

- *Respect & Listening:* Respect grounds good leadership. Respect flows from the basic dignity of all human beings. Respecting a person or one-self acknowledges the person's worth. To achieve this acknowledge-ment, the leader needs to cultivate the ability to be present to another person in a full human sense. This fundamental aspect of ethical rela-tions anchors and models the quality of relations among people in an organization. Respect flows out in contagious relationships across groups and reinforces cultural norms based around self-respect, respect for the task and purpose as well as the people served.

  Respecting and being present to people means leaders and manag-ers listen to others. The capacity to be present to another person and acknowledge them means really listening to colleagues, staff, subordi-nates and stakeholders. Respectfully being present invites others to give honest and candid assessments of actions and plans. Respect makes personal and organizational learning possible as well, as it asks deeper commitment from people to the mission of the organization. It invites serious collaboration, better contributions and, not just "buy-in," but enhanced responsibility and performance. Listening becomes the major modality by which leaders learn from others. If they listen with open presence, they actually hear the full range of emotional and intellectual content of other people's voices and not just translate other's commu-nications into their own worldview.

  Active and disciplined efforts to open one's mind and be present off-sets the tendency toward isolation that inheres in position and power. Managerial leaders can strive to create space for quiet and listening that encourages staff and stakeholders to speak accurately about challenges and to not hide problems and failures. Listening requires respect but grows from presence and openness that is revealed in a willingness to be curious and ask questions or let others ask questions. Often the hid-den challenges are waiting upon the right questions to ferret them out from disciplined listening.

- *Communication:* Respect and trust lead naturally to open and mutual communication. Communicating is critical to infusing the mission into actions, ensuring competence and creating accountability and commu-nity deliberation. This is another critical strategic dimension of ethical managerial leading. It flows from respect, creates trust and augments prudence and judgment.

  Managers begin by setting clear expectations that establish the norms of performance and over time set the organization's culture. Setting these norms requires persistent attention to communicating and listen-ing to see if the communications are heard and enacted. Managers need to fight isolation and get out to see and hear what is actually occurring and being understood. They need to cultivate multiple lines of reporting and wide ranges of listening and learning to understand the full range of actions and cultures in the organization.

Communication flows many directions. Any effective communication to other people depends upon respect and listening that enables leaders to understand people as an audience with their own values and modes of understanding. This approach permits leaders to cast communication in terms that can be apprehended cognitively and emotionally. At the same time, communicating, listening and learning leads naturally to leaders becoming involved in community deliberation with stakeholders and served communities to learn the real impact of policy. Managerial leaders need to discover the lived knowledge at the point of task performance.

To encourage rich communication and learning, managerial leaders need to strive to generate organizational environments where individuals can honestly communicate the reality of work life and express dissent in a productive way. On an individual level, this means actively working to avoid isolation and to break through the distortion fields that self-interest and deference can generate around them. Leaders can create practices of questioning or different forms of meeting, and above all protecting and rewarding, dissent and truthful insight.

Institutionally, individuals need to struggle to understand not just the known unknowns but also the unknown unknowns. This moves beyond individual efforts to system wide adaptations. This may involve building strong parallel systems of communication or accountability. It might require whistleblowing protection or ensuring that dissent has multiple points to express itself without fear of reprisal. Well-designed and confidential fraud, waste and abuse hotlines or good whistleblower processes and protections are needed to gain deep and accurate knowledge of the internal workings of the organization. They can provide protected opportunities to discover and engage unethical, illegal or inefficient operational challenges. These systems not only build trust and commitment but also ensure a better knowledge base and better decisions. They can provide antidotes to codes of silence, dominant informal actors and dangerous subcultures that can develop without strong mutual communication.

- *Fairness:* Fairness grows from a commitment to respect and equal dignity. Its practice can build strong relations across staff and stakeholders. It elicits compliance and commitment from personnel, clients and stakeholders. Respect grows from treating others with fairness and competence. Respect involves an active willingness to learn from and acknowledge others' concerns even if one does not agree with them. It involves the capacity to escape from one's preferred framework. At the same time, fairness involves a real commitment to communicating the logic of decisions. Too often, sub-cultures or groups will misinterpret the intent of a decision and this will cascade into deep distrust. Managerial leaders need to convey the reasons and logic behind actions and link them to fairness in order to both build legitimacy but also anticipate the predictable spin and misunderstandings that will accompany any hard decision.

One aspect of fairness in leading and managing requires persons to possess the ability to stand back and acknowledge, understand and use the frameworks that other people bring to the table. In this light, fairness demands a commitment to treating situations and actions consistently. But it requires leaders to delve deeply into the situation so they understand the full context and can act with fairness and explain their actions in a public way.

Fairness augmented by respect helps managers and supervisors naturally include diverse points of view into their deliberations and address sensitive issues of race, religion, class, and gender that arise in daily interactions. Fairness combined with respect infuses a strong cultural commitment to help individuals grow from mistakes. These combined approaches enable leaders to include all kinds of individuals in a common purpose and forge a shared culture across differences. Respect-based learning does not just identify the wrong done, but it provides people with clear and supported opportunities to practice effective ways that are reinforced by the manager. If personnel do not trust the fairness of managers, they will have strong motives to hide actions and avoid accountability or honest communication.

- *Impartiality:* Impartiality sustains trust and fairness. Being impartial for a leader does not mean treating everyone exactly the same, but it does require managers to use the same standards in evaluating individuals and situations. These standards need to be transparent and appealable. It also requires that managers explain their decisions in light of shared public standards so people understand why an action or policy affects them in a particular way. This reinforces the expectations and norms managerial leaders are building in a culture. It also reinforces the legitimacy of the organization in its relations to stakeholders.

If people believe that managers and supervisors play favorites and use different standards to evaluate certain personnel or situations, people will justly feel disrespected, resent supervision and punish the favored ones in informal ways. If they believe that other stakeholders are privileged and get special treatment they will resist action and resort to subterfuge to evade unfair treatment. People victimized by unfairness and favoritism will be more open to disengaged performance or blandishments to give special treatment to others.

Impartiality and fairness create foundations of strong group dynamics and trust. They build legitimacy and respect for an organization's decisions even if the decisions adversely affect one. Trust and respect build up social resources with staff and citizens that ease enforcement, make accountability more accurate and earn managers the benefit of the doubt and loyalty in difficult situations. Bonds of mutual reliance are strengthened by the confluence of impartiality, fairness, respect, communication and trust. These weave the connections of resilient teams and organizations.

If managerial leaders fail to generate trust, respect and communication, they open opportunities for outsiders to take advantage of internal managerial vacuums. They warrant resistance to the organization's actions. Lack of trust, aggrieved feelings of being ignored, feeling hopeless with no chance to communicate or impact decisions, or being treated unfairly—all provide traditional motives for individuals who sell out to provide information or services to outsiders or consciously neglect their performance.

Embrace Discretion

Integrity and responsibility converge for leaders in embracing their discretion and reveling in the possibilities open to creative use of the ethical imagination. Good managerial leaders excel at fitting the imperatives of position and organizational standards to the complexity of an unfolding incident or complex challenge. This approach offsets the temptation for managers and supervisors to hide behind rigidity and forget their discretion and responsibility even as they exercise them. They are tempted to see themselves as doing nothing but "applying the rules," with no personal judgment involved. This retreat from integrity avoids the pain of complex and imperfect judgments and deflects accountability for consequences. Yet every manager or supervisor constantly exercises discretion. It anchors the honor and responsibility of good leaders.

- *Frames:* Human judgment depends upon cognitive frames that integrate cognitive, perceptual and emotional aspects of the mind. People use stereotypes to scan and identify significance in situations because stereotypes are efficient and based upon experience. When grounded in self-aware reflection and practice, frames emerge as the essence of trained professional judgment. People act from frames that shape the world they perceive and code information to provide fast and trained assessments of reality.

This means that all managers exercise discretion at the very moment of what they see and do not see; what they hear and do not hear; and how they code the importance of their observations. While selective perception arises from the frameworks managers hold, it can lead to decisions that miss different points of view or new aspects of a relevant situation. Unreflective discretion can easily lead to decisions based on limited, biased and preconceived judgments. Knowing and compensating for one's frames is a central ethical prerequisite of good leading.

- *Pervasive Discretion:* The application of rules and regulations inevitably involves discretion. Leaders even employ discretion in the amount of time they devote to different topics or people; this allocation of time in turn signals to others the relative importance of people and issues. Often situations involve multiple rules, and sometimes the rules conflict.

The resolution of this conflict usually requires important decisions by managers on the application and interpretation of different rules. Consequently, managers need to be particularly attuned to the perceived fairness of their execution of discretion. For instance, a simple conflict between a subordinate and superior over choice of language could be interpreted as harassment, an insult, good supervision, bad judgment, immaturity or oversensitivity. The choice of which interpretation or rule to apply will determine the severity of the incident as well as avenues of action for those involved. In addition, managers and supervisors possess the choice of whether to write up the incident and, if so, how to describe the incident. In each of these judgments, they not only define the incident but also focus on the relevant values they want to defend or support and the culture they are building. Managers and supervisors constantly exercise judgment and discretion and must be aware of this. It is the key to both acknowledging responsibility and training their judgment to address the complexity of situations.

Protect the Core

Government and nonprofit organizations arise from public purposes that play out as the performance of core activities that give substance to the mission. They engender a suite of responsibilities that are critical to achieving the goals and tasks of institution. These core functions and responsibilities become the fundamental stewardship obligations of managerial leaders. They involve not just the suite of tasks and functions but also the social capital essential to long-term performance of functions.

The obligation to build and sustain the core functions covers a range of vital areas under the ethical ambient of managerial leaders. These obligations require absolute attention to the competence and performance of personnel and the monitoring of the effects of actions. They scale from the very basics of managing the hiring, promoting, firing and personal development of personnel to resolute attention to the finance and budget of an organization. The personnel embody the expertise necessary to execute the responsible tasks. At the same time, the ethical focus extends to ensuring that the organization has not just the requisite level of expertise but also information and if necessary the scientific evidence to guide and justify decisions. This encompasses ensuring strong analytic capacity to assess and guide decisions based upon the information and evidence.

Many government organizations are tasked with providing not just reliable service but also credible information and data that stakeholders and sometimes whole sectors of society and the economy rely upon to guide their own actions. They are charged to provide a reliable and accepted database stakeholders can use in their relations with each other. Underlying the provision of service and information lies the responsibility to deepen the resilience or robustness of an organization, especially in the public sector where it might be the only organization providing critical services to vulnerable citizens. This also extends to a wide range of scientific and information services that governments provide, upon which the entire economy and society often depend as reliable and unimpeachable sources of actionable knowledge.

The example of providing credible and accepted information points to another critical aspect of the organizational core managerial leaders should attend to. Leaders must manage the reputation and reliability of the agency. The trust in an organization's credible expertise is essential for effective and accepted government performance. This involves not just sustaining credible information and expertise but fighting to sustain plausible neutrality or at least nonpartisan information and practice. These responsibilities require constant attention to both internal management and controls, but also guarding the boundaries of the organization to guarantee that the agency is not captured by a stakeholder. A public organization will lose immense influence and tasks will become much more difficult if it is perceived to be running a privately controlled agenda instead of legally mandated and accountable tasks.

Engage the Whole Context

If every situation was clear and simple, and managers and supervisors were all knowing, then discretion would not be necessary. Managers and supervisors could just apply the rules by rote, assuming they could evaluate what rule to apply and how to weigh it compared to other rules. In many cases, they could just use a decision algorithm to minimize uncertainty or inconsistency. Life is seldom so simple. Managerial leaders always face incomplete information; multiple sometimes-conflicting stories of what happened; several relevant regulations; and issues of power, legitimacy or identity overlaying the decision-making stakes. Acting well to build support for long-term organizational action obligates leaders to develop strong situational awareness.

Making decisions without attending to the entire range of consequences, as well as the lasting impact to competence, culture and legitimacy of decisions, involves a form of ethical negligence given the obligations of an official position.

- *Open to Multiple Frames:* One of the first obligations of leaders is to discover as much as possible about a situation. This flows from the obligations of being prudent and effective as well as commitments to honesty and respecting diversity. This goal requires that leaders leave behind their own de fault framework of perception and judgment and seek multiple ways to understand a situation. They must know the full political, scientific and social context in which it occurred. As is always the case with good leading, managers need to use their imagination and use multiple frameworks to understand a situation and exercise judgment. What sounds like racial epithets could be banter? What looks like assault could be roughhousing? What appears initially to be negligence could be two goals in conflict? What looks like lack of common sense may involve deeper knowledge of unanticipated consequences? Knowing the people involved and the context is critical for the manager to address an issue and to teach staff how to successfully resolve pressing organizational matters. Thoughtful leaders pause, stand back and map out all the actors, their perceptions and the stakes that entangle any incident and account for them to achieve competent, fair and self-disciplined solutions.

Model and Educate

Every action of a managerial leader puts their power and authority on the line. People around them are always watching and reading their words, intentions and actions. The one thing managerial leaders have true control over is their own actions and modeling. Leaders earn respect and trust or disrespect and distrust in this daily crucible. The power of managers over their people's futures and resources can distort how staff, clients and others react to managers. The more senior one is, the greater the distortions of behavior and information. This places a greater onus on managers to provide clear and consistent signals and direction for people.

Managers and supervisors carry the culture of the organization. They represent and affirm the values and mission of an organization. In the political space between organizations or units that collaborate to achieve purposes, individuals express these values and interests as they negotiate and adjust among partners and adversaries to persevere in the goals and sustain the capacity of the organization's mission.

Inside and outside the organization, managerial leaders make a difference whether they believe it or not. Their cumulative actions, praise, support or nonsupport and punitive actions educate people on organizational expectations. The contagion effects of the leaders impact the quality of energy and commitment of people. If they inspire trust and respect, they can have a profoundly positive influence on the values and performance of their employees. Poor or indifferent managers and supervisors damage morale, undermine values and discourage staff commitment and achievement. Continuous ineffective or bad managing contributes to suboptimal performance, disengagement and lack of trusting cooperation. These actions alienate stakeholders and erode the credibility of one's organization or group. Day after day, each incident and decision provides an opportunity to define the meaning of a situation and set norms or precedents that contribute to the long-term direction and culture of the organization.

Exercise Courage and Endurance

The daily press of organizational life demands a continuous and stressful stream of judgments and actions from a conscientious managerial leader. The cumulative force of isolation, peer norms, rigidity, secrecy, disruptive individuals and diversity tensions can exhaust the moral resources of even very capable individuals. Sheer routine can dull one's awareness of the cumulative importance of daily decisions. It requires sustained courage to go to work day after day and take responsibility for hard decisions, attend to routine decisions, adjust to changing circumstances and deal with success, failures and well-intentioned mistakes. Responsible managers are always tempted to rigid rule compliance, blaming others or evasion of responsibility, or they surrender control to dangerous informal actors or wrong-headed superiors. Giving in relieves individuals of the stress and pain of making hard decisions but also of acknowledging and addressing mistakes or adverse consequences of actions.

Leaders and managers generate fields of influence and control around their authority and actions. People closely follow the actions over time. Reliable and consistent performance creates strong expectations among staff and citizens. One-time actions will not build culture or credibility, and inconsistency or emotional blow-ups can lose hard-earned trust and credibility in one fateful moment. Sustained, fair and consistent performance, even in face of obstacles and resistance, is the only way to win respect and trust and send the message that the values the manager enacts must be taken seriously. Only then will the culture of groups change, and norms become imbedded in daily actions.

This means courage in small things can be very consequential because if others sense a flagging commitment, low-level hypocrisy or favoritism, rumor networks will proliferate and undermine a manager's credibility and ability to motivate or lead. Good managers persevere and figure out how to adapt and renew ethical commitment and direction in spite of the inevitable resistance and obstacles that will arise. Enduring commitment and sustained action are hard and require self-aware discipline and efforts to build a support team. This strength and daily courage over time can help build a culture and norms for people; one's courage signals to personnel that a leader has their back. This endurance can model and rally the support needed to make values real in the daily lives of individuals.

Seek Support and Help

All solutions and actions in organizations result in imperfect and incomplete resolutions of issues; this is the way of life. Managers frequently address murky and messy problems. Sometimes they will make mistakes; often they will fail in achieving their full goals. Facing ethically fraught and complicated results of actions is physically, psychologically and ethically arduous. Leaders are often second-guessed or attacked for their actions. They need to reflect and learn from their actions and figure out ways to keep their dedication and persistence alive. As a result, managerial leaders need to remember they are not alone in facing uncertainty or dilemmas. If they try to make it alone, ultimately, individuals will encounter emotional and physical exhaustion and burn out from the daily grind.

Managerial leaders need friends, allies and peers to sustain their integrity and commitment. Multiple sources exist for gaining support or help in keeping integrity and dedication intact. Support can become important for job longevity as well as clarity of thought and decisiveness. Superiors, respected colleagues, peers and mentors can be important sources of support and help. Professional networks and networks of friends are critical to provide forums for candid and honest advice. People outside of one's workplace provide a forum to vent, reflect and often find renewal for one's purpose.

Managerial leaders, especially as they rise in authority, need to take care not to bring everything home to their family or make family their sole source of support; it places too great a burden on family life and can undermine vital intimate relations. If the problem is with a superior or with the peer culture, human relations offices, bargaining units or outside control agencies such as human rights offices or the Inspector General's Office can provide assistance or anonymous reporting processes. In the long run, leaders need to build networks of trusted associates such as friends and peers with whom they can share the strains and joys of the office and find intellectual and emotional support for work.

Bibliography

Adams, G. B., & Balfour, D. L. (2009). *Unmasking administrative evil* (3rd edition). Armonk, NY: M. E. Sharpe.

Anechiarico, F., & Jacobs, J. B. (1996). *The pursuit of absolute integrity: How corruption control makes government ineffective*. Chicago, IL: University of Chicago Press.

Ashkenas, R. (2017, February 2). How to overcome executive isolation. *Harvard Business Review Newsletter*.

Bazerman, M. H., & Tenbrunsel, A. E. (2011). *Blind spots: Why we fail to do what's right and what to do about it*. Princeton, NJ: Princeton University Press.

Bertok, J. et al. (2005). *Public sector integrity: A framework for analysis*. Paris, France: OECD.

Bolman, L. G., & Deal, T. E. (2011). *Reframing organizations: Artistry, choice and leadership*. New York, NY: John Wiley & Sons.

Christensen, C. M., Allworth, J., & Dillon, K. (2012). *How will you measure your life?* New York, NY: Harper Collins.

Cohen, S., & Eimicke, W. (2002). *The effective public manager: Achieving success in a changing government* (3rd. edition). San Francisco, CA: Jossey-Bass.

Cooper, T. L., & Wright, N. D. (Eds.). (1992). *Exemplary public administrators: Character and leadership in government*. San Francisco, CA: Jossey-Bass.

Dobel, J. P. (1993). The realpolitik of ethics codes: An implementation approach to public ethics. In Frederickson, H. G., & Ghere, R. K. (Eds.), *Ethics and public administration* (pp. 158–176). Armonk, NY: M. E. Sharpe.

Dobel, J. P. (1999). *Public integrity*. Baltimore, MD: Johns Hopkins University Press.

Dobel, J. P. (2005). Managerial leadership and the ethical importance of legacy. *International Public Management Journal, 8*(2), 225–246.

Dobel, J. P. (2007). Public management as ethics. In Ferlie, E., Lynn, Jr., L. E., & Pollitt, C. (Eds.), *The Oxford handbook of public management* (pp. 156–181). Oxford, UK: Oxford University Press.

Dobel, J. P. (2015). What athletic achievement can teach about ethics. *Public Integrity, 17*(4), 319–330.

Elliston, F. et al. (1984). *Whistleblowing: Managing dissent in the workplace*. New York, NY: Praeger.

The European Ombudsman. (2003). *The European code for good administrative behavior*. Luxemburg: Office for Publications of the European Communities.

Frederickson, H. G. (1997). *The spirit of public administration.* San Francisco, CA: Jossey-Bass.

Frederickson, H. G., & Ghere, R. K. (Eds.). (2013). *Ethics in public management* (2nd edition). Armonk, NY: M. E. Sharpe.

Goodsell, C. (2011). *The mission mystique: Belief systems in public agencies.* Washington, DC: CQ Press.

Goodsell, C. (2015). *The new case for bureaucracy.* Washington, DC: CQ Press.

Grant, A. M. (2013). *Give and take: A revolutionary approach to success.* New York, NY: Penguin.

Huberts, L. (2014). *The integrity of governance: What it is, what we know, what is done and where to go.* Basingstoke, UK: Palgrave Macmillan.

Huberts, L., & Hoekstra, A. (Eds.). (2016). *Integrity management in the publics sector: The Dutch approach* (pp. 146–158). The Hague: Bios.

Janis, I. L. (1982). *Groupthink: Psychological studies of policy decisions and fiascoes.* Boston, MA: Houghton Mifflin.

Jurkiewicz, C. L. (2006). Power and ethics: The communal language of effective leadership. In Frederickson, H. G., & Ghere, R. K. (Eds.), *Ethics in public management* (pp. 95–113). Armonk, NY: M. E. Sharpe.

Jurkiewicz, C. L. (Ed.). (2015). *The foundations of organizational evil.* London, UK: Routledge.

Kouzes, J. M., & Posner, B. Z. (2006). *The leadership challenge* (Vol. 3). New York, NY: John Wiley & Sons.

Kouzes, J. M., & Posner, B. Z. (2011). *Credibility: How leaders gain and lose it, why people demand it* (Vol. 244). New York, NY: John Wiley & Sons.

Lewis, C., & Gilman, S. C. (2005). *The ethics challenge in public service: A problem solving guide.* San Francisco, CA: Jossey-Bass.

March, J. G., & Olsen, J. P. (2010). *Rediscovering institutions.* New York, NY: Simon and Schuster.

Milgrim, S. (1975). *Obedience to authority.* New York: Harper Torchbooks.

Moberg, D. J. (2000). Role models and moral exemplars: How do employees acquire virtues by observing others? *Business Ethics Quarterly, 10*(3), 675–696.

Moberg, D. J. (2006). Ethics blind spots in organizations: How systematic errors in person perception undermine moral agency. *Organization Studies, 27*(3), 413–428.

OECD. (1998). *Principles for managing government ethics.* PUMA Policy Brief. Retrieved May 12, 2017 from: www.oecd.org/puma/gvrnance/ethics/index/htm

OECD. (2000). *Trust in government: Ethics measures in OECD countries,* Paris: OECD.

Rainey, H. G. (2014). *Understanding and managing public organizations* (5th edition). San Francisco, CA: Jossey-Bass.

Sabini, J., & Silver, M. (1982). *Moralities of everyday life.* New York, NY: Oxford University Press.

Schein, E. H. (2009). *The corporate culture survival guide.* San Francisco, CA: Jossey-Bass.

Schein, E. H. (2010). *Organizational culture and leadership.* New York: NY: John Wiley & Sons.

Senge, P. M. (2006). *The fifth discipline: The art and practice of the learning organization.* New York, NY: Doubleday.

Transparency International. (2011). *National integrity system: Background rationale and methodology.* Retrieved March 2, 2016 from: www.transparency.org/files/content/nis/NIS_Background_Methodology_EN.pdf

Tudnem, R., & Burnes, B. (Eds.). (2013). *Organizational change, leadership, and ethics.* London, UK: Routledge.

Visser, H. (2016). Integrity incorporated in strategy and daily processes: The Netherlands Tax and Custom Administration. In Huberts, L., & Hoekstra, A. (Eds.), *Integrity management in the public sector: The Dutch approach* (pp. 146–158). The Hague: Bios.

Weick, K. E. (1995). *Sensemaking in organizations* (Foundations for organizational science). Thousand Oak, CA: Sage Publications Inc.

5 Leadership Values

Managers are the ethics teachers of their organizations. They leave a legacy of people they influence for good or bad. Whether managers intend to teach or not, they deeply influence the ethical life of the organization, and people will be better or worse because of their presence. It comes with the territory. This reality means managerial leaders embody stewardship of the ethical values and mission of the organization.

This range of values elaborates the cognitive and emotional architecture needed to embrace values and mission and then promise to act upon them. They describe the ethical dispositions, character attributes, virtues and values that persons need to commit to values and norms and guide decisions and implement actions based upon them. They present an internal checklist for oneself to examine one's own actions or when balancing a team's composition and ethical capacity. They recall and deepen the understanding of character attributes and values mentioned in Chapters 2 and 3 on public integrity and leading.

This range of values and character traits serves as a reference point in the space of self-reflection. Being aware and attending to the values and character attributes permit individuals not only to assess their own ethical stances but also to consider what they should focus on in educating and managing the organization. Different situations may require different weights for values, such as courage or fidelity for line regulators facing recalcitrant businesses who try to resist or bribe them, or the need for honesty and accounting in ensuring that line staff facing unreasonable quotas are not tempted to compromise reporting records. Understanding and reflecting upon the range of values permits an evolving weighting and fit with situational demands.

Managers and leaders are obliged to self-consciously exhibit the foundational values of their institutions. In doing this, they need to model the basic ethical dispositions and practices that operational values and culture depend upon. These cumulative concerns come home to a set of values that leaders need to enact as the basis of their leading.

These values must be relentlessly stated and modeled at the senior level and reinforced all the way down to the supervisory level. If the values and mission only exist at the top in an unread "mission statement," they are meaningless and become sources of disenchantment, scorn and cynicism. These values anchor daily self-aware leading.

This constellation of values explains the dispositions, temperaments, virtues and articulated values that individuals must possess to act with sustained commitment to values when facing adversity and the daily friction of organizational life. This listing consolidates dimensions that are mentioned throughout this analysis. They pull forward aspects of integrity and managing a culture and build a psychological scaffolding for persons and groups to sustain the emotional and cognitive clarity and strength to act. Recalling these values and traits makes them inner cognitive and emotional resources for people. Individuals can recall and focus upon them as a source of motivation; as a focus for perception and scanning a situation; and as a standard to guide decision making. They provide emotional and ethical weight to the standards a person deploys.

Key Leading Values

- Integrity
- Responsibility
- Fidelity and Courage
- Competence
- Respect
- Truthfulness and Honesty
- Accountability and Transparency
- Inclusiveness
- Stewardship

Integrity

This is the lodestone value for this approach to managing and leading. The human self with integrity comes down to the idea that a person has the ability to form a conception of self and guide actions based upon that conception. Integrity flows through adopted, trained and internalized frames of judgment and action. It depends upon self-awareness and the ability of a person to stand back and generate an idea of a desired end. The person can exercise internal discipline and focus to overcome internal and external obstacles and arrange attention, energy and time to act to further the intent. Integrity coupled with responsibility means a person seeking goals for good reasons can control, set aside or channel internal emotions and demands that resist their purpose. Integrity depends upon a level of ethical and character consistency across the actions and growth of a person. It enables people to make and keep promises that ground the ethics of managerial leading.

Integrity expresses itself as the ability to exercise disciplined judgment in light of values and dispositions for the mission. Integrity builds on self-control and the ability of individuals to use constrained judgment for intentional purpose that focuses the will to act. The individual has the ethical ability to adopt the discipline of reflective action by training their understanding and perception of situations through practice and learning. This practice results in cognitive frames in their minds. The frames guide them to concentrate attention and perception by attending to each dimension of responsible public leading. Good experienced leaders can process organizational situations with efficient and timely perception and assessment of situations. This ethical link is deepened because intentional leading results in ethical consequences in the world. Operational integrity, then, is an activity that people practice to integrate cognitive, emotional and physical activities expressed as trained habits of judgment and action.

Responsibility

Good leaders promise to live up to the obligations and demands of a position within a mission or organization. They must self-consciously work to acknowledge their positions of authority and the obligation to fulfill the responsibilities of their position, including the relevant laws and regulations. The human mind will constantly default to positions that deny moral responsibility or avoid complex and disruptive information. Self-awareness of responsibility is critical to avoid these traps.

This extends integrity to its twin virtue of responsibility. Responsibility relies upon the self-discipline to live up to promises and hinges on the honest willingness to acknowledge one's contributions to actions and not retreat to self-deception, the world of blame games or passing the buck. Being responsible gives action more ethical value. Possessing responsibility leads actors to acknowledge the joy and satisfaction of achievement as well as the moral pain and recrimination that accompanies failure, mistakes or negligence. Responsible presence opens the person up to the full range of situational awareness and the need to both learn and carry on.

Fidelity and Courage

Fidelity requires courage, and this means that individuals have the self-discipline and moral strength to faithfully live up to their promises to uphold the law, principles and values necessary to do the job ethically and legally.

They manifest as the ability to overcome temptations and impulses. Fidelity plays out as the capacity to decide and act consistent with the integrity-based values and commitments. The reality of any position of official responsibility is that obstacles will emerge, work will grind down commitment and people will offer blandishments to act with less than highest steadfastness to regulations and intent of the task. Fidelity and courage align in small daily actions and in larger actions to build consistency and sustainable expectations into a culture. Fidelity sustained by courage is fundamental to build trust among workers as well as assured relations with stakeholders and the public.

Competence

The entire project of public and nonprofit organizations depends upon missions to achieve vital public purposes. Achieving the missions through tasks and cooperation with each other in and across organizations requires knowledge and skills—the competence—to achieve the necessary tasks. Citizens, colleagues and partners are enmeshed in a web of dependence and reliance that rely upon the competent performance of tasks by each other. Entire chains of performance and communities of practice build upon mutual reliance on the competence of colleagues and leaders. The obligations to master the requirements of a position are fundamental to leaders and to how they manage their people.

Competent individuals possess the skills, training and capacity to do their defined jobs. It places an added obligation to keep up these skills and moral capacities in order to adapt to changes and demands of the job. People should be hired and trained in light of their potential competence, and doing so is a fundamental requirement of leaders. Competence requires caring about the small details of organizational life that give reality to the larger mission. Citizens, colleagues and collaborators depend upon the competence of leaders and this reinforces the moral obligations of reliance upon competence.

The idea of competence aligns powerfully with a commitment to responsibility. Being responsible places a heavy obligation upon a person to master the skills and knowledge content of a job and to understand the context of performance. A responsible leader takes on the obligation to know the requirements of a position and focuses attention, energy and time to learn the skills required to achieve a goal, but also the more complicated commitment to self-correction. This competence commitment is reinforced by respect for the position, the intricacy of the task, the people who rely upon it and for oneself and one's promise. Others cannot make a person better; the individual leader must undertake this effort exercising judgment for themselves and demanding it of personnel. This emphasizes the cognitive and ethical aspects of any position. A person seeks not just to master the position but also to get it right.

Respect

The recognition of dignity based upon equal human dignity is the foundation of respect. It is, in turn, anchored in self-respect and requires leaders to treat all humans with civility and appropriate honesty. Respect can infuse all expectations giving them a strong moral cast beyond just webs of reliance. Respect entails legitimate demands for competence and improvement from individuals and is anchored in being present to others, listening and learning. It reinforces commitments to competence and responsibility.

Truthfulness and Honesty

One of the most enduring ethical aspects of effective and responsible leading lies in a commitment to honesty and truthfulness about performance. Ethical reflection requires honest self-assessment and avoids self-deception. Effective leadership requires that managers understand the full context and facts in any given situation; this requires truthfulness and honesty in leader–follower relationships. Eliciting honest and candid reporting depends upon people trusting that a manager and leader will use the information to address needed issues and further the mission and not use information to harass or punish individuals or groups.

A trusted commitment to honesty encourages people to report clearly and accurately task expectations and the methods by which people will be held accountable. Only when honesty is valued can a true learning environment exist. In this context, mistakes can become a way of learning how to improve performance rather than an opportunity for evasion and duplicity. Truthfulness also involves a commitment to not be trapped in one framework and to understand the entire context of incidents and actions.

Honesty and truthfulness are even more vital because the tendencies of the human mind and of groups soften or hide disconfirming or painful information. The human mind prefers consistency in its evaluation and possesses the ability to confirm its own biases and be influenced by proximate affirmation. People tend to overestimate their own knowledge and undervalue other sources who differ from them. Successful persons often resist disconfirming evidence, deny responsibility or generate endless blame or excuses. Groups can close together, and groupthink reinforces closed conceptions of assessment and denies information or reinterprets it to fit their predispositions. It takes conscious and tenacious effort and modeling for oneself and teams to ensure that individuals seek out and engage the best information possible, even if it challenges one's prejudices or points to one's shortcomings. Truthfulness and honesty ally with a dedication to transparency as a critical ethical antidote to the tendency of groups and individuals to distort or deny information that might threaten their interests or agency.

Accountability and Transparency

Transparency expands and heightens the fundamental obligation of public agencies to be accountable to citizens, and nonprofit organizations should be accountable to their donors and funders and more broadly their communities. Inertia and self-interest will propel organizations to protect their self-understood purposes and interests by controlling information. The control or distortion of information allies with many other dimensions of the human mind's defaults that protect underperformance or goal displacement. Managerial leaders need constant attention to pushing for transparency in performance and information in order to ensure learning in the organization but also accountability to the public purpose and authorizers.

Transparency and accountability can also be allied in efforts to be inclusive and reach out to communities and stakeholders and bring them into the deliberative process of decision making. Community alignment and engagement become natural extensions of transparency and accountability for organizations. In addition, transparency opens up active dialogue with stakeholders and authorizers and creates the possibility of much more informed and proactive change driven by community energy and ideas. Transparency opens mission up to reform and adaptation.

Active oversight and honest and accurate reporting of what really happens in institutions enables government and nonprofit authorizers to delegate responsibly to organizations. The legitimacy of public and nonprofit organizations depends upon accurately understanding what is really happening and whether an organization is actually achieving goals consistent with its mission. Accountability justifies strong financial control systems and programs such as ethics hotlines or well-designed confidential reporting systems to ensure accurate knowledge and safe reporting of illicit and dangerous activity that can escape normal accountability processes and scrutiny. Accountability permits institutions to revise missions, grow and improve in response to feedback and evaluation of programs and services.

Inclusiveness

Public organizations require ethical attention to all internal and external stakeholders as well as constant adaptation to changes in the political and social environments. The radar of good managerial leaders maps both internal and external environments and recognizes all significant actors in the political environment. In addition, commitments to the public good, mission and respect often require leaders to ferret out groups who are not obviously well organized or powerful and to include them in deliberations and assessments of the organizations.

Seeking out and understanding the points of view of stakeholders makes policy and leading more sustainable and less coercive. The obligation to include flows from respect, fairness and stewardship to address the long-term needs of institutions and society. At the same time, deep economic, identity and gender divisions stalk every public purpose in terms of achieving the mission as well as building a strong common organizational culture committed to a public purpose. Managerial leaders need to pay specific attention to such economic, cultural and identity aspects in order to create policies sensitive to often hidden dimensions of implementation. In addition, leaders must address these differences among class, race, gender and religion in the ongoing effort to build responsive and committed organizational culture.

Organizations need multiple, professional skill sets which come with their own preferred ways of looking at the world. Leaders must ensure that no one professional view dominates, and they must build a team with balanced decision capacity. As a value, inclusiveness inoculates against the deep human tendency to be comfortable only with people who are similar. It also guards against the tendency to judge individuals by stereotypes or appearance rather than their full human capacity. It protects people from slipping into their default frames of reference when judging situations and helps them expand their imagination and deploy multiple frames of reference to engage problems and people. It contributes to stronger and more effective decision making, but requires consistent leadership, sensitivity and support.

Stewardship

Organizations and leaders are not given money, power and resources to pursue their private ends or gain. Nor are they charged with vital purposes to fail. Each managerial leader inherits an organization or team, works there for a while and then moves on, leaving the organization and its resources in place for future leaders and enduring missions. Organizations endure after managerial leaders leave. The challenges and problems they are designed to address remain. Good managerial leaders serve as stewards of the long-term purposes of an organization as well as the capacity of the organization to achieve them. They work to build the capacity as well as achieve the goals so that the long-term purpose remains intact.

Using money as efficiently as possible and not wasting funds does justice to the unique characteristics of taxable or donated funds. Managers and leaders have special obligations that inhere in the requirement to spend the public funds for authorized purposes. Taxed funds are coercively taken for public purposes, and special obligations of efficient and transparent spending follow this coercive taking. Donations are voluntarily given from people's wealth for specific purposes, and this donative decision also places special burdens on efficient and accountable expenditures. The financial and budgetary aspects of stewardship are critical responsibilities both for legitimacy and to achieve goals. Stewardship means public service leaders attend to the long-term welfare of the institution and staff rather than simply respond to short-term demands and trends. As stewards, they fight to build and protect core knowledge, skills and support for the mission and organization. As one aspect of their stewardship, managerial leaders are responsible to hand on institutions that possess competence and legitimacy, and these become vital ethical considerations in leading.

Bibliography

Bailey, S. K. (1964). Ethics and the public service. *Public Administration Review*, *24*(4), 234–243.

Bruce, W. (2001). *Classics of administrative ethics*. Boulder, CO: Westview Press.

Burke, J. P. (1986). *Bureaucratic responsibility*. Baltimore, MD: The Johns Hopkins University Press.

Ciulla, J. B. (2003). *The ethics of leadership*. Boston, MA: Wadsworth.

Cooper, T. L. (1987). Hierarchy, virtue, and the practice of public administration: A perspective for normative ethics. *Public Administration Review*, *47*(4), 320–328.

Cooper, T. L. (2006). *The responsible administrator: An approach to ethics for the administrative role* (5th edition). San Francisco, CA: Jossey-Bass Publishers.

Dobel, J. P. (1990). *Compromise and political action: Political morality in liberal and democratic life*. Savage, MD: Rowman & Littlefield.

Dobel, J. P. (1990). Integrity in the public service. *Public Administration Review*, *50*(3), 354–367.

Dobel, J. P. (1998). Political prudence and the ethics of leadership. *Public Administration Review*, *58*(1), 74–81.

Dobel, J. P. (2007). Public management as ethics. In Ferlie, E., Lynn, Jr., L. E., & Pollitt, C. (Eds.), *The Oxford handbook of public management* (pp. 156–181). Oxford, UK: Oxford University Press.

Elliston, F. et al. (1984). *Whistleblowing: Managing dissent in the workplace*. New York, NY: Praeger.

The European Ombudsman. (2003). *The European code for good administrative behavior*. Luxemburg: Office for Publications of the European Communities.

Farazmand, A. (1997). *Ethics, professionalism and the image of the public service: A report*. New York, NY: U.N. Secretariat.

Gawande, A. (2010). *Checklist manifesto*. New York, NY: Penguin Books.

Geuras, D., & Garofalo, C. (2010). *Practical ethics in public administration*. Management Concepts Inc.

Gracian, B. (1993). *The art of worldly wisdom* (C. Maurer, Trans.). New York, NY: Doubleday.

Hart, D. K. (1974). Social equity, justice, and the equitable administrator. *Public Administration Review*, *34*(1), 3–11.

Hougaard, R., & Carter, J. (2017, December 19). If you aspire to be a great leader: Be present. *Harvard Business Review Newsletter*.

Kahneman, D. (2011). *Thinking, fast and slow*. New York, NY: Macmillan.

Macaulay, M., & Lawton, A. (2006). From virtue to competence: Changing the principles of public service. *Public Administration Review, 66*(5), 702–710.

Machiavelli, N. (1997). *The prince* (R. Adams, Trans. & Ed., 2nd edition). New York, NY: Norton Critical Editions.

Milgrim, S. (1975). *Obedience to authority*. New York: Harper Torchbooks.

Moberg, D. J. (2000). Role models and moral exemplars: How do employees acquire virtues by observing others? *Business Ethics Quarterly, 10*(3), 675–696.

Moberg, D. J. (2006). Ethics blind spots in organizations: How systematic errors in person perception undermine moral agency. *Organization Studies, 27*(3), 413–428.

Nagel, T. (1978). Ruthlessness in public life. In Hampshire, S. (Ed.), *Public and private morality* (pp. 75–92). Cambridge, UK: Cambridge University Press.

O'Leary, R. (2006). *The ethics of dissent: Managing guerilla government*. Washington, DC: CQ Press.

Price, T. (2008). *Leadership ethics: An introduction*. Cambridge, UK: Cambridge University Press.

Rohr, J. A. (1986). *To run a constitution: The legitimacy of the administrative state*. Lawrence, KS: University of Kansas Press.

Rohr, J. A. (1988). *Ethics for bureaucrats: An essay on law and values* (2nd edition). New York, NY: Marcel Dekker.

Rohr, J. A. (1999). *Public service, ethics and constitutional practice*. Lawrence, KS: University of Kansas Press.

Senge, P. M. (2006). *The fifth discipline: The art and practice of the learning organization*. New York, NY: Doubleday.

Stivers, C. (1994). The listening bureaucrat: Responsiveness in the public service. *Public Administration Review, 54*(4), 364–369.

Sun-tzu. (2006). *The art of war* (J. Minford, Trans.). New York, NY: Penguin Books—Great Ideas.

Terry, L. D. (2003). *Leadership of public bureaucracies: The administrator as conservator* (2nd edition). Armonk, NY: M. E. Sharpe.

Transparency International. (2011). *National integrity system: Background rationale and methodology*. Retrieved March 2, 2016 from: www.transparency.org/files/content/nis/NIS_Background_Methodology_EN.pdf

Tudnem, R., & Burnes, B. (Eds.). (2013). *Organizational change, leadership, and ethics*. London, UK: Routledge.

6   Unethical Behavior and Ethical Slippage

A leader and manager in a government or nonprofit organization possesses strong ethical obligations to provide high quality performance based on the conferred mission. This grant of authority, resources and power authorizes individuals to ensure that tasks are performed consistent with the authorization of power. It also requires assessment of the consequences to certify that the actual impact of the organization aligns with the sanctioned purposes. The ethics of managerial leading in these organizations entails living up to the obligations of regulations and procedures but also filling in the silence and interstices of the regulations with actions guided by the mission purposes and basic leadership values.

These positions involve a public trust. In exercising leadership, ethical behavior should not be conflated with legal behavior, but the two are intimately linked. Law and accountability legitimize public institutions. Nonprofits depend upon a web of laws and complex terms of delegation and expenditure from boards, communities and donors. Managerial leaders embody and represent these values to personnel, citizens, authorizers and the outside world. Clear illegality violates the moral premise of managerial leadership. Deeper ethical behavior, however, involves understanding the reasons behind the law and being a steward of these in the context. It means being aware of and combating the "threats to integrity" and the institutional vulnerabilities that undermine professional ethics, quality performance and personal integrity in daily life. This requires relentless attention to the "threats to integrity" that erode daily performance and faithfulness. The values and character displayed by managerial leaders in the gaps or silence of law or rules is essential to guiding the quality of people's ethics.

Beyond the threats to integrity, common classes of unethical behavior pervade public and nonprofit organizations. Managerial leaders need to be acutely aware of the scope of behaviors to recognize, anticipate and address. Three of the most common and relevant classes of unethical behavior involve: 1) violations of trust; 2) self-dealing; and 3) conflicts of interest.

While separate categories, they often overlap and in some cases, each of these behaviors may be present. Many behaviors are embedded in small seemingly innocuous decisions like allocating excess resources for a project or helping a friend at the expense of the team or putting off distasteful decisions to address an underperforming or abusive subordinate. A superior can order someone to lie, look the other way or misreport. Managers might promote someone not qualified in the interest of serving his or her own ideological or personal agenda. A managerial leader needs to resolutely search out these behaviors and act decisively to address them. This section lays out the range of anticipated challenges that leaders need to watch for.

Just as the list of leadership values and character can be recalled as an inventory of moral resources, a catalogue of unethical behaviors and how they manifest can serve as a vital ethical asset. This inventory enables individuals to fine tune awareness of these issues and concentrate attention on the signals and behaviors around them. This self-awareness and inventory of ethical challenges complements daily managerial leadership to prevent, uncover and address ethical slippages.

Range of Unethical Behavior

- Violations of Trust
- Self-Dealing
- Conflict of Interest

Violations of Trust

As stewards of public and nonprofit missions, individual leaders carry a public trust to pursue the organization's purpose. Protecting and furthering these entrusted responsibilities explain many of the unethical actions to monitor. The trusteeship expresses itself as stewardship obligations to build the organization and achieve the mission with skill, respect and effectiveness. More specifically, violations of trust can occur through incompetence, abuse of power, lying, favoritism, disrespect, discrimination or inappropriate silence or evasion. The following sections provide explanations of these actions and the obligations to address them.

- *Incompetence:* Competence is the building block of organizational ethics. The achievement of a mission and its subsequent impact on the world and lives of human beings involves a chain or circle of reliance between the welfare of citizens and colleagues to the reliable and competent performance of tasks. All people in a sequence of dependency presume that people in an organization or partnership have the capability and will to do the job.

Indifference to quality of performance and failure to address incompetence generates a cascade of consequences to the world and welfare of citizens who depend upon services or the safety of food, water, air or buildings. Internally, incompetence snowballs into a hidden distortion of information or cumulative poor decisions, or it foists debilitating extra workloads on others, undercuts overall effectiveness and engenders resentment and cynicism. Besides monitoring, correcting and helping people get better, this difficulty expresses itself through the obligation to hire and promote the most qualified individuals and not use inappropriate standards that place non-competent individuals in positions of responsibility.

• *Abuse of Power:* Individuals are entrusted with positions and official power on the understanding that they will use their power in a way that serves agreed upon common ends in agreed upon ways. Unethical action in organizations often involves the abuse of power and position. Individuals let their personal interests or beliefs override the mandate's purpose. Self-interest, prejudice or ideological affinity dominate their decision; they exploit entrusted responsibility and power for their own ends. Such actions, even when legal, are still wrong. Actions may be by individuals or supported by group norms that protect or encourage wrongdoing.

Using excessive physical or non-physical force to achieve the organizational goals is abuse of power and reinforces threats to integrity. Most government tasks implicitly rely upon the controlled deployment of force to achieve goals, from taxation to regulation to public safety, so it becomes a special concern of government action.

The raw use of physical or psychological coercion to achieve goals undermines staff and personnel, engenders greater hostility and resistance from clients and citizens and requires much higher levels of oversight. Physical and psychological abuses often stand behind extortion or threats to gain personal or political ends not sanctioned by the organization. They can also be used to cover up actions. Unmanaged force degrades humans by violating their dignity. Permitting bullies of citizens or staff encourages abuse of power and loss of managerial control. Removing competent and committed officials because they did not accede to a superior's personal or ideological bidding at the expense of legal, procedural and institutional standards corrupts the authority and competence of the organization.

• *Lying:* The legitimacy and performance of public organizations depends upon transparency and accountability to ensure that actions align with public purpose. Lying, the corruption of good information and hiding or falsifying information threatens the core integrity of public organizations and leadership. Passing on or forcing personnel to pass on distorted information or deliberate untruths to colleagues, superiors or subordinates is lying. Another variation is covering up or withholding information individuals need in order to do their jobs. Spreading untrue or inaccurate information about policy or others within or outside the organization poisons the culture of honest evaluation and accountability.

Lying distorts the ability of the organization and managers to understand exactly what is occurring in the organization. It cuts accountability off at its roots and makes high performance impossible. It can channel performance into unproductive or failed patterns. If mistakes are covered up and not acknowledged, individuals cannot grow and learn, and greater institutional disasters easily unfold. Bad information and failed policy or processes can become deeply imbedded and hidden in organizational practice leading to suboptimal performance and tragedy. In a world of partnering and collaboration, lying and misinformation destroy the critical but often fragile trust necessary across collaborators even with shared purposes. The distrust eats away at the heart of collaborations to achieve any durability.

- *Favoritism:* Favoritism involves special treatment of individuals that violates consistent and professional standards of treatment. It can cover denial of rightful benefits or provide illicit benefits to personnel or stakeholders. Favoritism in regulation creates an unfair playing field for stakeholders and undermines compliance and respect for law. Favoritism damages equity and fairness and engenders disrespect. Internally, favoritism such as unearned promotions or benefits undermines competence, trust and legitimacy. At a cultural level people come to believe that that professional excellence does not get rewarded, but going along with superiors' wishes regardless of content does. Favoring or protecting a friend, an identity affiliate or political favorite often enables and encourages lying, incompetence and abuse of power. Favoritism encourages a culture of cliques and obeisance to individuals with power; the will to curry favor displaces the ambition to excel. Favoritism breeds webs of connection that subvert performance driven missions and cultures.
- *Disrespect:* The deep structure of public ethics is built upon a commitment to human dignity, and the dignity drives the importance of the value of respect. Respect supports innumerable aspects of managerial leadership ethics. Respecting oneself produces the drive to master the

requirements of a position. In addition, self-respect informs the power to make and keep promises. Respect for oneself drives respect for the position and produces high performance in one's task and for managing people to achieve their own self-respect and achievement. Personnel arrive at self-respect through purpose and achievement in their jobs, and this creates a virtuous loop for culture, people and tasks. At the same time, respect for people's dignity buttresses the obligation to conscientiously perform one's task.

Disrespect disconnects one's integrity from one's self-awareness, concern for workers and teams as well as the people who depend upon high quality performance. Disrespect means citizens and staff are treated in ways that violate tenets of civility, truthfulness and competence. Disrespect plays out in policy process that ignores or devalues the community and people served. Internally it can disguise itself as respect. Too often managers mistake respect for not telling the truth or avoiding the hard decisions that are required for organizations and people to grow. They fear "hurting" people or causing inefficiency or disruption in the organization. In fact, being honest to others is a strong act of respect that permits people and organizations to know their success, failures and perceptions of others. Disrespect effectively ends strong learning within an organization by undermining the ability to listen and the willingness of people to risk speaking candidly or commit to the organization's purpose. A culture of disrespect makes it extremely difficult for individuals to sustain their commitment to the organization's mission and can lead to resistance and illegitimacy with the citizens supposedly served by the organization.

- *Discrimination:* Equal dignity and a commitment to developing high-performing individuals are deeply wounded by discrimination. Discrimination violates the dignity of people by judging them based on attributes such as race, religion, gender or appearance rather than mandated performance standards. Judging on the basis of such imbedded characteristics violates the right of a human to be assessed on the basis of character, values and performance. Discriminating this way violates the manager's own promise to abide by the standards and processes of a position. Discrimination can be systematic and unseen by people in organizations and can lead to differential treatment to whole classes of people in impact of implementation or internally in recruitment, training and promotion. Implicit bias can permeate a culture and become unseen and normalized. It takes strong leadership efforts to identify and address these patterns. Such discrimination makes inclusive and honest decision making very difficult; in addition, it lowers performance, invites conflict, becomes a flashpoint for conflict and lawsuits and destroys the capacity of teams to function together.

- *Silence or Looking the Other Way:* Silence always beckons as a threat to integrity and ethics because it poses an easy way out, a way to avoid hard actions and moral pain. Silence can mean people collude in or permit unethical or illegal action by pretending not to see it, not reporting it or going along with inappropriate peer behavior. Codes of silence gain strength because they entangle personal loyalties to coworkers and friends with abetting corrupt actions. It cuts at the heart of any sense of co-responsibility for an organization's actions and missions. It undermines any sense of shared contribution and shared accountability. This can include superiors who perceive such behavior in their area of responsibility and choose to not rectify the problem, as well as individuals who go along with illegal or immoral orders and do not seek ways to educate, voice dissent or change policies within the system over time. Silence becomes a habit that enables normalization of deviance and broken cultures to take root and spread. This silence can protect colleagues, friends or feared bullies. It can reflect broken and alienated relations to work where a person's loyalty has migrated to self-interest and group rather than mission. Codes of silence are the main weapon corrupt cultures and actions depend upon to flourish.

Self-Dealing

Individuals self-deal when they use an official position to gain benefits for themselves or others that are beyond the legitimate benefits and compensation accorded officials in that position. Self-dealing poses particular dangers because most individuals will self-deceive themselves that the self-dealing does not compromise their actions and impartial judgment. People possess strong capacities for self-deception about their involvement in corruption and convince themselves that their judgment will not be subverted or they are really doing good when corrupt. In addition, self-dealing enables outside groups or individuals to capture organizations for their own purposes or distort an equal playing field for stakeholders.

This type of unethical behavior can have an especially pernicious effect on an organization by undermining the purpose and fairness of organizational performance in an unaccountable manner. If left unchecked it becomes contagious and encourages other personnel and stakeholders to embark on their own corrupt behaviors. Self-dealing can involve several types of behavior that often interlock such as: bribery, theft, inefficiency, collusion and kickbacks.

- *Bribery:* Providing special treatment for individuals in a person's realm of responsibility in exchange for some form of personal or professional gain for the official who grants the treatment. This can involve wide ranges of sophistication from simple "gifts" or promises of employment for oneself or others or to guarantees of contracts that benefit oneself indirectly through a shell company. The benefits can be time delayed, hidden by off shore or complex financial dodges or migrate to family and friends rather than the person. The exchange can involve anything from privileged access to information, biased decisions or inaction in the face of regulatory violations. In most people's minds, bribery is the archetype of corrupt behavior where a person or organization serves the private purposes of an actor on a quid pro quo basis.
- *Theft:* Taking organizational resources that should be devoted to a mission purpose and using them for personal usage or gain. This can include theft of resources or time. Sometimes it begins in an unassuming way by taking equipment home from work, taking extra time on breaks or using work supplies to supplement income. These small actions can grow into a sense of entitlement that becomes a larger systemic problem. It can be aggravated when personnel across the organization amplify the cost, such as when taking extra time on breaks across the organization or taking home supplies become huge money and time losses. Theft is often hidden behind favoritism or laziness, personal business on organization time or stealing time from the task at hand. Theft can scale up to corrupt practices such as misemployment of government assets by using staff for personal work or giving away government resources or privileges such as licenses for less money. Often the theft is linked to a form of bribery gain.
- *Inefficiency:* Using excessive amounts of resources to achieve an end that could have been accomplished with fewer resources. It can be a pervasive organizational problem that can range from purchasing unneeded equipment to paying excessive fees for supplies, contractors or performance. Internally, favoritism or unearned promotion or acceptance of incompetent individuals leads to lack of return for investment on mission purpose. It can cover wasting organizational time on personal tasks to permitting incompetent staff to continue while others cover for them. Many modern inefficiencies arise in contracting out the use of third party consultants with opaque financial arrangements. It violates the stewardship obligation to maximize welfare from the resources entrusted to leaders and managers and undermines the legitimacy of the organization in the eyes of tax paying citizens and funders.
- *Collusion:* Cooperating with other individuals, including contractors or network partners, to make funding decisions that are inefficient or allocating resources to provide excessive gain to the contractor, partner or individuals. It can encompass channeling resources to private pur-

poses rather than mission aims. The collusion can cover a wide range of sophisticated and often hidden behaviors such as paying far more than market value for performance of services, narrowing the circle of bidders for public performance, working with shell organizations or giving privileged information or access to help outsiders gain contracts or warrants.

• *Kickbacks:* Accepting some form of payment from an individual, partner or contractor in exchange for favorable decisions to allocate resources to them. Kickbacks and related behaviors are deeply implicated with collusion or anticipated bribes or inefficiencies. They can often be hidden as side payments to actors related to an organization's officials or hidden by shell companies. They undermine competence, stewardship, efficiency and impartiality and fairness.

Conflict of Interest

Persons with conflict of interests decide or act in circumstances where the individual official or those related to the individual stand to materially benefit from a decision or action. The entangled interests of the decision makers then distort their decision in ways that undermine the common good or mission of the organization. Conflicts of interest are often denied by individuals believing that their own integrity will overcome perceived conflicts, but the reality is that individuals skew their decision making over time to support these outside interests. Most professional and agency Codes of Ethics focus their energy on these issues and bribery. Nepotism and similar situations, where spouses, friends or relations report to each other, jeopardize the integrity of accountability. It also arises when individuals have a proprietary interest in an organization with whom they are partnering, contracting, negotiating or doing business. Shell companies can be used to hide these gains to officials or their associates and family.

Conflicts of interest are so dangerous because the officials deny they exist even as everyone else knows they distort decisions. Future employment possibility with a firm that the official regulates or conducts business with create them. Nepotism and conflicts of interest undermine the quality of judgment and the perception of inclusiveness and fairness. Known conflicts of interest degrade equal treatment of stakeholders and clients and incentivize actors to curry favor with officials rather than act on the basis of merit or public criteria. Perceived conflicts of interest undermine the trust of stakeholders in the reliability and fairness of decisions. They destroy stakeholder belief in fair judgment and equal playing fields. Like collusion, bribes and inefficiency, conflicts of interest are linked to private actors seeking to minimize risk and maximize gain in relation to public and nonprofit organizations. They incite cycles of corruption internally and externally toward the organization.

Patterns of Ethical Vulnerability and Slippage

- Vulnerability and Slippage Points
- Point of Task Performance
- Internal Elements
- External Elements

Vulnerability Points for Unethical Behavior and Cultures

Building an ethical and high-performing culture means more than inculcating high standards of performance and decision making. A good managerial leader needs to get ahead of the possible erosion of value-based performance in organizations. The ethical leader has obligations to seek out, identify and address where the greatest pressures on individuals and culture will occur and proactively buttress individuals, policy and structure to tackle them. This anticipation is the key to sustaining ethics for the long term in corrosive and shifting political environments.

This means understanding the range of unethical behavior and how it arises. For example, unethical behavior does not always begin with a bribe; it begins with a small favor. Selling out does not often happen suddenly in one decision, but emerges slowly within a web of relations that traps or blinds a person to the real moral stakes. Managerial leaders build positive culture by personally displaying leadership values and norms that model values. They model and support personnel to give people the strength to act on those values when under stress. They not only model the values but also set boundaries and coach others to understand the boundaries as well as provide effective ways to act upon value commitments. Even when it seems arduous or silly, the capacity of individuals over time to fall into self-deception about their relationships means that managerial leaders need to be especially mindful of small things that delineate their responsibilities and prepare personnel to identify and deal with those who seek to gain something from them.

This responsibility puts high pressure on officials to live up to the standards because their actions really do model behavior or undermine their message with hypocrisy. Individuals can take home "perks" from the office and signal to everyone that this is okay. Minor silences or white lies smooth over irregularities in reporting and make it possible to seem to meet impossible targets. The laws and rules are often silent or contradictory and leave room for considerable discretion. Proper exercise of discretion can address and prevent many smaller unethical behaviors that seep out slowly, infect others and corrupt a culture.

Managerial leaders need to actively identify and seek out the slippage points and intervene to reinforce ethical and competent behaviors before erosion of individuals and cultures occurs. These slippage points and strategic management interventions involve understanding the main resource base of organizations, the internal pressure points upon performance and the external pressure points upon performance. Each pressure point becomes a focus of strategic managerial leadership action.

- *Culture:* Unethical action usually occurs at an individual level, but such actions often reveal a culture of distorted values or corruption. Studies point out that systematic corruption tends to arise in situations that mimic monopoly power that involves discretion without strong accountability. This can occur in government agencies but also in nonprofits that may serve as the fulcrum of service delivery for public purposes. This means unethical behavior can reflect badly designed structures, training or incentives where demands of performance conflict with the need for professional autonomy, sufficient resources or self-interest. Unethical behavior imbedded in culture becomes both invisible and self-sustaining. Managerial leaders need to pursue holistic responses to anticipate and address issues.
- *Vulnerability Points:* Organizational susceptibility to unethical behavior and corruption follows from a number of identifiable problems. The problems often arise at the point of task performance from internal and external pressures upon the individuals performing the tasks. This occurs when actors encounter an asymmetry of stakes between external actors engaging internal officials. These stresses upon individuals arise usually from nexus points where external stakeholders perceive high stakes or high gains from influencing the official behaviors of people. They are aggravated when the people performing the actions do not have sufficient training or management support from a combination of lax or limited oversight, badly designed incentives or mismatches between obligations, resources and external pressures. Deeper corruption can occur when the senior decision makers are captured by external actors or act for their own benefit; at this point, the entire organization can become corrupted in its purpose even if many persons within it act with honor and competence.

A number of different but often overlapping situational variables come together to create organizational vulnerability points. They usually involve stresses upon individuals who are trying to do the right thing under great pressure from external or internal forces pushing against them. These continuous stresses fracture their commitment. The predictable tension points between the obligations and status of the individual performing the task and internal or external pressures create points of vulnerability that can be identified and can become a managerial focus.

Knowing these focal points ensures that managers can focus attention, resources, design structures and incentives to support public service values in the organization and anticipate the patterns of performance standard erosion. Senior executive and especially appointed or elected officials can also pressure senior management leaders to manipulate their power and the direction of the organization in order to meet the leader's personal or external group's goals rather than mandated public purposes. At this point, the entire system grapples with corrupt pressures upon senior officials. This requires a far more aggressive external campaign to build scrutiny of the organization and support for agency independence.

- *Focus Elements:* The following table identifies predictable points of potential strain and slippage of the organization's values and accountability. Each focus element and each point of contact between them can overlap and increase the pressures. Great inequality in power can generate these situations, such as when underpaid personnel try to enforce regulations but face a powerful and well-connected external actor. This tension can be aggravated by differences in professional status, race, gender, religion, class or training. In a similar way, the peer norms of an organization's task groups could support high values or have evolved to either collude with external actors or get around unrealistic quotas for performance with shortcut behaviors or subverted reporting.

Each of the following elements becomes a potential leverage location for managerial leaders to attend to and build the culture and ethics of an organization because they can anticipate and focus energy upon predictable problem sites. This approach highlights how managerial leaders can identify and

Table 6.1 Management Leverage Points for Ethical Slippage

Point of Point of Task	Internal Elements	External Elements
• Authorized Power	• Managerial Attention	• Stakes for Actor
• Mission Commitment	• Expectations	• Power of Actor
• Training/Expertise	• Peer Norms	• Inequality
• Discretion	• Inequality	• Differences
• Technology	• Differences	• Number of Interactions
• Resources/ Compensation	• Boundary Management	• Contractors/Competitors/ Partners
	• Technology	• Funding

uncover slippage points. It also identifies the array of resources and nexus points they can engage to confront the issues and manage the boundaries of integrity and performance and challenges to public ethics.

Point of Task Performance

- *Authorized Power*: Most public and many nonprofit agencies possesses sole, exclusive or primary authorized power in areas of service provision, convening deliberation around issues, information provision, regulation, permitting or certification. The stature of power and the exclusive authority give an immense institutional, legal and ethical importance to these organizations. They amplify the ethical, social and economic stakes for individuals and stakeholders who deal with the organizations. The stakeholders face serious consequences from the decisions of these organizations and have powerful incentives to seek to influence, change or capture the decisions of these organizations. Leaders need to be relentlessly aware that the power of their organization invites endless external scrutiny and pressure, and the lack of competition can encourage inertia bound or subverted performance. Shoring up power to address significant power differentials with outside actors becomes a vital task for managing boundaries of organizations and supporting task performance.

- *Mission Commitment:* Individuals' commitment to mission values to guide their judgments heavily depend upon the clarity of their understanding the rules of their position informed by the core mission values. This understanding is inculcated and reinforced by follow-through on constant communication and reinforcement through hiring, evaluation and promotion. This structure of communication and support helps individuals act with commitment and skill in their jobs on a sustained basis. A commitment is reinforced by managers who set clear expectations and enforce the boundaries and do not permit lingering low-level slippage or corruption. Personnel need to be confident that they will be supported by senior managers when they make hard decisions that protect public value yet aggravate private interests. This focus addresses the quality of integrity and commitment possessed by people in the organization at the point of task performance. Declines in commitment to mission within personnel can deeply impact the quality of independence of performance.

- *Training/Expertise:* The level of training or expertise for the individuals at the point of task performance is critical to deal with workloads, challenges, surprises, differences in competence levels and working with group and organizational differences. Professional competence can increase personnel's comfort with the technologies deployed in doing their jobs. These elements extend management attention to everything from ensuring a solid knowledge base to recruiting and hiring to evaluation, promotion and incentives. The level of professional skill addresses vital issues that can arise when dealing with powerful and rich stakeholders as well as ensuring skilled and respectful treatment for the less powerful. Any gaps between the expertise needed to perform a task and people's competence, or between the skill levels of personnel and external actors, places stress on integrity performance.

- *Level of Discretion:* The range of discretion for individuals should influence the level and intensity of training for professional competence and the necessary oversight and political support. These imperatives of support rise, as discretionary decisions can involve significant stakes for external stakeholders. The relative power or lack of power of external actors who interact with the person performing the task profoundly impacts the quality of performance. Individuals with little power might face very high stakes such as arrest or access to welfare benefits, which amplifies the power of organizational personnel. At the same time, organizational personnel might deal with external actors with great political or economic power in areas such as regulating a building code, protecting public health or the environment. The wider the discretion of an official combined with the greater the stakes or inequality of power of external actors generates immense ethical stress.

- *Technology:* The level of technology deployed by personnel may change constantly, whether it involves information systems, performance measures, forms to be filled out, questions that must be asked, practiced judgment under high stress situations or the range of issues examined in certifying or granting a permit or eligibility. Public and nonprofits often undertake tasks that require significant skilled judgment, analytic reasoning, evidence-based judgment, strong information management and professional implementation or systematic evaluation. This creates a strong imperative to keep up the technology mastered by organizational personnel, especially in light of how policy challenges can permute or stakeholders can adapt to new regulations. Any division between the skill and training of personnel and their technology or between the technology demands and the demands of superiors or the environment can place great stresses upon values and performance. Powerful and rich actors can often bring to bear high-level technology and resources to resist or deflect regulation or enforcement and organizations need to respond in kind.

- *Resource Level:* Sufficient resource support is absolutely critical for individuals who are performing important tasks. At the most fundamental level, guaranteed and adequate compensation is critical to maintain adequate skilled personnel pools and to reinforce the ability of personnel to resist unethical blandishments to subvert their tasks to benefit private interests. Adequate resources, compensation and training all grow in importance when the organizational tasks involve high stakes for external factors such as regulation, permitting, public safety, advocacy or providing critical services for vulnerable and needy clients. The resource level can play out as training, information, expertise and skills necessary in the arms race between regulators and stakeholders in many domains of public policy. Personnel who are underpaid, undertrained and not well supported are fundamentally more vulnerable to being suborned or abusing power with external actors. Sometimes they can simply be overmatched by the expertise and resources of the stakeholders. Resource support becomes an essential bastion against self-dealing, external pressures for favors or internal pressures for compromised service.

Internal Elements

- *Attention:* Attention is the most precious resource a leader possesses. A manager's attention and time signals the importance of issues to personnel and stakeholders. The constant press of daily business and endless surprises can distract attention and undermine the flow and consistency of policy decisions. The amount of managerial support, attention, oversight and monitoring is critical to high performance in environments of political and ethical stress. Leaders need to calibrate their attention and energy in light of both the internalized integrity and training of personnel but also in light of stresses imposed by external environmental pressures. As stresses and stakes go up, the organization needs to invest in scanning for signals of ethical slippage and corruption. This enables leaders to apply more integrity design and incentive analysis as well as training and consistent managerial attention at stress points.
- *Expectations:* All organizational tasks carry expectations. Authorizers and funders regularly resort to performance measures and assessments to establish accountability through expectations. Modern governance is deeply implicated in contracting, and setting and managing expectations. Internal demands to produce outcomes with increasingly limited resources and still justifying organizational missions relative to other priorities can drive organizations to impose top down quotas upon performance. These quotas and evaluation criteria often have no relationship to the resources required to perform the tasks or the complexity of

the challenges. Unrealistic performance expectations and measures can generate immense stress upon task performance. If the personnel do not believe that the goals actually measure the good they seek, or if the goals require actions that exceed resources or training, or if the goals do not match the complexity of the environment, these stresses can cause personnel to take shortcuts, subversive actions or distort reporting to "meet" the goals.

These challenges impose obligations upon managerial leaders to manage goal expectations internally and often to manage up against unrealistic demands of authorizers and funders. This is especially important if understaffed or overworked personnel face higher work-loads with reduced funding or have to address a more difficult problem set while being required to achieve more. This can also lead to peer group expectations and informal group norms developing to support subverted accountability and performance.

- *Peer Norms:* Peer norms develop in any group performing a task over time. These norms help establish a sense of identity and belonging, shape morale and commitment, regulate performance levels and provide hidden and informal sanctions and rewards for members. Peer norms can also arise to protect groups from unrealistic expectations or address unsafe or dangerous working conditions in areas such as public safety, corrections or mental health. They can also hide and support ethical slippage and groupthink.

  Managerial leaders have a pervasive responsibility to learn and influence these peer and informal norms. The group norms become central to an organization's value culture. They buttress integrity, expertise and group solidarity. They bolster organizational resilience and can strengthen organizational ability to weather harsh pressures from external actors seeking to undermine standards or get special treatment. If not managed well, however, peer norms can subvert values by embodying accommodations to unrealistic expectations, low training and compensation or collusion with external actors who are willing to suborn people to get desired treatment.

- *Inequality:* Internally or externally, significant inequalities of power between organizational personnel and served citizens or external actors can cause immense stress upon ethical performance. Many public and nonprofit organizations have deep obligations to serve justice considerations to ensure equal respect and care across issues such as generational justice, environmental protection, public health or public safety. For example, the stress could occur when people of one class or race conduct social service intake interviews for vulnerable clients of a different race class. Another form might involve the regulation of building permits or health inspections where undertrained or low paid personnel attempt serious task performance with limited resources and confront external actors with superior skills, resources, power and political influence. Actors with significant external power will use networks of support to bring pressure upon the mission and capture performance to support their interests. The inequality can run across many fault lines from class to ethnicity to geography to gender differences. As strains rise or overlay, they impose immense stresses upon integrity driven value performance. Managerial leaders need constant attention to monitoring the boundaries of performance where differences and inequality collide. At the same time, they need to invest in influencing the external political environment to build support to ward off or counter external power networks and support their staff and mission.

- *Differences:* Intense performance stresses can arise when the inequality of office or power is amplified by systematic differences among people. Differences of class, race, gender, geography, ethnicity or religion seem the most obvious, but professional differences and expertise can aggravate decision making as well. Tensions over understanding the mission and perceived fairness and respect can arise when different self-identified groups work together. Misunderstandings can escalate if the lines of authority reflect identity differences. Issues become even more complex if many of those regulated are of one identity group, while the regulators are of another identity group. The issues around differences extend to managing different working or learning styles or professional background. Being aware of these latent difference challenges and actively anticipating and addressing them in organizational building and culture require constant attention.

- *Boundary Management:* The boundary lands at the point of task performance or intersections of accountability with authorizers, poses constant tensions between mission integrity and the desires of external actors to influence an organization to act for their benefit. These same boundary land intersections can engender regular abuse of power by organizations over populations who are regarded as hostile or different or possess little power and social status. Attending to the boundary lands with unswerving efforts to learn exactly what is happening as well as investing attention and resources to reinforce competent, fair and effective performance is vital. This requires strong accountability and communication measures. Managerial leaders also need political awareness and actions to bolster both internal competence, culture and fairness as well as efforts to influence the political environment in a way that supports personnel against efforts to suborn them.

- *Technology:* Technology can be a vital motor for effective service and extending the capacity of public personnel to perform well. In technical regulatory areas, acquiring, training and deploying the best available knowledge, expertise and physical tools is critical to dealing with the complexity and power of modern business and production methods. Modern technology also provides a much stronger set of methods to monitor accountability and insulate actions from corruption and cooptation. Installing and using these technologies becomes a powerful means to support integrity and performance, bolster transparency and ward off incessant efforts to subvert the mission.

External Elements

- *Stakes:* External actors with high stakes in organizational decisions often push to gain special treatment or access from a public purpose organization. These external organizations or individuals can be very powerful external actors seeking special treatment for their issues, and they may deploy economic, political or social connections to pressure people. Often the stakes for them are very high and time sensitive, so they push the boundaries of engagement with public regulators. The asymmetric stakes can also arise for poor individuals who face threat of incarceration or service denial, which would lead both groups to attempt bribes to change behavior. Organized crime and cartels combine the worst of both aspects in how they seek to corrupt public organizations. When the stakes are higher for the external actor than for the organizational personnel, the external actors will be tempted to press for advantage or privileged treatment or access given their stakes in the outcome. The high stakes for the external actors can be aggravated if there are pronounced differences in class, race, gender or ethnicity between the officials of the organization and the clients or citizens at the point of interaction. When external actors or clients perceive the stakes as high, managerial leaders need to devote considerable attention to support and monitor the daily intersection points. They can expand these efforts to provide resource support for staff, engage the political environment to educate, persuade external stakeholders to change behavior or invest in a range of managerial resources to expand support.
- *Power, Inequality and Differences:* The greater the wealth and power of external actors or clients, the more complex and difficult these interactions become. The mirror image of external actors are clients with little power and great differences within the organization. This situation poses the challenge of organizational abuse toward them. The values of fairness, competence, efficiency, integrity and accountability all come

to bear in regulating activities or providing services. Often those with wealth and power are central to a community or organization's wealth or revenue stream; they can influence considerable political networks and mobilize external authorizers to bring pressure upon organizations. Managerial leaders need to develop prudent and effective strategies to generate the external political support needed to sustain the performance and autonomy of their organization and to provide competent and impartial service in these environments. A mirror strategy exists for ensuring respect and competence toward unequal but vulnerable or dependent populations, which can involve both strong internal management coupled with efforts to match organizational personnel more demographically closer to the served and active outreach to communities involved.

- *Interactions:* Even something as simple as the number and quality of interactions needs to be managed. Technology can replace many compromised interactions. One-time interactions provide more opportunities for slippage in performance because no long-term, face-to-face accountability will occur. These service interactions can seem random yet reveal over time significant patterns of possible discrimination or slippage in respect or competence. The arbitrary nature of one-time encounters requires special attention to ensure fair, effective and respectful treatment. More numerous interactions create incentives for more respectful, efficient and competent behavior. Repeated interactions, however, can also generate informal relationships and expectations that could subvert fair or competent performance. Long-term interactions can also lead to aggressive extortion actions by public personnel as in shakedown behavior or aggressive stakeholder behavior designed to intimidate or wear down personnel such as safety inspectors in high-risk industries. Each set calls for different types of ethics management.
- *Competitors/Contractors/Partners:* Competitors for the organizational mission or even partners, allies or contractors can, themselves, pressure individuals and organizations to perform in ways to maximize the competitors' or partners' or contractors' share of a market or network. The world of collaboration increases the range of the possibility for collusion, pay to play, bribery, kickbacks and conflicts of interest in partnering or outsourcing. These pressures can occur in nuanced ways from political pressure, opaque bidding relationships or conflict of interest issues. They can be hidden in obscure contract provisions or manifest in hiring or recycling people through closed networks or patterns of moving in and out of sectors with anticipated future employment opportunities influencing judgments. These pressures place special obligations upon managerial leaders to develop competencies in contract writing

and manage common purpose and accountability across multiple organizations. Managerial leaders need to attend to the transparency of network and partner relationships as well as focus heavily upon managing the integrity of hiring and relationships with partners and networks.

- *Funding:* Modern governance leads many public and nonprofit institutions to manage multiple and complex funding streams. These can range from legislative allocations to bonding to grants to fees for service. Managerial leaders need to manage the integrity of funding streams and purposes as well as ensure quality financial management and transparency. The more complex the funding strategies and the increasing need to use capital markets requires huge management investment in quality personnel and financial control systems create transparency to address the complex and risky decisions and hidden fee structures that complex financial transactions can mask.

  Constant slippage can arise when organizations face short-term revenue shortfalls or changed demand that can tempt managers to shift resources across dedicated revenue streams to others to accommodate short-term needs. Transparent auditing, financial controls and management of financial relationships and funding becomes even more important to match the statutory and funding obligations. Many nonprofits can be overmatched by the complexity of financing schemes compared to their resource personnel base. Each of these opens new tension points for internal fraud or where funders can seek illicit gains for decisions in modern governance networks. Reciprocal and long-term funding or contracting relationships must be maintained, but they also become standing points of potential favoritism, excessive fees and loss of accountability due to complexity of financial arrangements. These relations require constant focus upon competent and transparent auditing and management to guard against serious ethical slippages.

Bibliography

Adams, G. B., & Balfour, D. L. (2009). *Unmasking administrative evil* (3rd edition). Armonk, NY: M. E. Sharpe.

Anechiarico, F., & Jacobs, J. B. (1996). *The pursuit of absolute integrity: How corruption control makes government ineffective.* Chicago, IL: University of Chicago Press.

Arendt, H. (1965). *Eichmann in Jerusalem: A report on the banality of evil.* New York, NY: Penguin.

Bardach, E., & Kagan, R. A. (1982). *Going by the book: The problem of regulatory unreasonableness.* Philadelphia, PA: Temple University Press.

Bazerman, M. H., & Tenbrunsel, A. E. (2011). *Blind spots: Why we fail to do what's right and what to do about it.* Princeton, NJ: Princeton University Press.

Bertok, J. et al. (2005). *Public sector integrity: A framework for analysis*. Paris, France: OECD.

Cohen, S., & Eimicke, W. (2002). *The effective public manager: Achieving success in a changing government* (3rd edition). San Francisco, CA: Jossey-Bass.

Dobel, J. P. (1993). The realpolitik of ethics codes: An Implementation approach to public ethics. In Frederickson, H. G., & Ghere, R. K. (Eds.), *Ethics and public administration* (pp. 158–176). Armonk, NY: M. E. Sharpe.

Dobel, J. P. (1998). Political prudence and the ethics of leadership. *Public Administration Review, 58*(1), 74–81.

Elliston, F. et al. (1984). *Whistleblowing: Managing dissent in the workplace*. New York, NY: Praeger.

The European Ombudsman. (2003). *The European code for good administrative behavior*. Luxemburg: Office for Publications of the European Communities.

Gawande, A. (2010). *Checklist manifesto*. New York, NY: Penguin Books.

Goldhamer, H. (1978). *The advisor*. New York, NY: Elsevier.

Goodsell, C. (2011). *The mission mystique: Belief systems in public agencies*. Washington, DC: CQ Press.

Goodsell, C. (2015). *The new case for bureaucracy*. Washington, DC: CQ Press.

Grant, A. M. (2013). *Give and take: A revolutionary approach to success*. New York, NY: Penguin.

Graycar, A., & Prenzler, T. (2013). *Understanding and preventing corruption*. Basingstoke, UK: Palgrave Macmillan.

Hirshman, A. O. (1970). *Exit, voice and loyalty*. Cambridge, MA: Harvard University Press.

Hougaard, R., & Carter, J. (2017, December 19). If you aspire to be a great leader: Be present. *Harvard Business Review Newsletter*.

Huberts, L. (2014). *The integrity of governance: What it is, what we know, what is done and where to go*. Basingstoke, UK: Palgrave Macmillan.

Huberts, L., & Hoekstra, A. (Eds.). (2016). *Integrity management in the public sector: The Dutch approach* (pp. 146–158). The Hague: Bios.

Jackall, R. (1988). *Moral mazes: The world of corporate managers*. Oxford, UK: Oxford University Press.

Janis, I. L. (1982). *Groupthink: Psychological studies of policy decisions and fiascoes*. Boston, MA: Houghton Mifflin.

Janis, I. L., & Mann, L. (1977). *Decision making: A psychological analysis of conflict, choice, and commitment*. New York, NY: Free Press.

Johnson, R. A. (2003). *Whistleblowing: When it works—and why*. Boulder, CO: L. Rienner Publishers.

Jurkiewicz, C. L. (2006). Power and ethics: The communal language of effective leadership. In Frederickson, H. G., & Ghere, R. K. (Eds.), *Ethics in public management* (pp. 95–113). Armonk, NY: M. E. Sharpe.

Jurkiewicz, C. L. (Ed.). (2015). *The foundations of organizational evil*. London, UK: Routledge.

Kahneman, D. (2011). *Thinking, fast and slow*. New York, NY: Macmillan.

Kaplan, R. S., & Norton, D. P. (2004). *Strategy maps: Converting intangible assets into tangible outcomes*. Cambridge, MA: Harvard Business Press.

Kellerman, B. (2004). *Bad leadership: What it is, how it happens, why it matters.* Cambridge, MA: Harvard Business School Press.

Klitgaard, R. R. (1991). *Controlling corruption.* Berkeley, CA: University of California Press.

Klitgaard, R. R., MacLean-Abaroa, R., & Parris, H. L. (2000). *Corrupt cities: A practical guide to cure and prevention.* Oakland, CA: Institute of Contemporary Studies Press.

Kornblum, A. N. (1976). *Moral hazards: Police strategies for honesty and ethical behavior.* Lexington, MA: Lexington Books.

Lewis, C., & Gilman, S. C. (2005). *The ethics challenge in public service: A problem solving guide.* San Francisco, CA: Jossey-Bass.

Light, P. (1995). *Thickening government: Federal hierarchy and the diffusion of accountability.* Washington, DC: Brookings Institution.

Milgrim, S. (1975). *Obedience to authority.* New York: Harper Torchbooks.

Moberg, D. J. (2006). Ethics blind spots in organizations: How systematic errors in person perception undermine moral agency. *Organization Studies, 27*(3), 413–428.

Moore, D. A., Cain, D. M., Loewenstein, G., & Bazerman, M. H. (Eds.). (2005). *Conflicts of interest: Challenges and solutions in business, law, medicine, and public policy.* Cambridge, UK: Cambridge University Press.

O'Leary, R. (2006). *The ethics of dissent: Managing guerilla government.* Washington, DC: CQ Press.

OECD. (1998). *Principles for managing government ethics.* PUMA Policy Brief. Retrieved May 12, 2017 from: www.oecd.org/puma/gvrnance/ethics/index/htm

OECD. (2000). *Trust in government: Ethics measures in OECD countries.* Paris: OECD.

Riordon, W. (1963). *Plunkitt of Tammany Hall.* New York, NY: Dutton.

Rose-Ackerman, S. (2013). *Corruption: A study in political economy.* New York, NY: Academic Press.

Rose-Ackerman, S., & Palifka, B. J. (2016). *Corruption and government: Causes, consequences, and reform.* Cambridge, UK: Cambridge University Press.

Rotberg, R. I. (2017). *The corruption cure: How citizens and leaders can combat graft.* Princeton, NJ: Princeton University Press.

Sabato, L. J. (1991). *Feeding frenzy: Attack journalism in American politics.* New York, NY: The Free Press.

Sabini, J., & Silver, M. (1982). *Moralities of everyday life.* New York, NY: Oxford University Press.

Schein, E. H. (2009). *The corporate culture survival guide.* San Francisco, CA: Jossey-Bass.

Schein, E. H. (2010). *Organizational culture and leadership.* New York: NY: John Wiley & Sons.

Stark, A. (2000). *Conflict of interest in American political life.* Cambridge, MA: Harvard University Press.

Sun-tzu. (2006). *The art of war* (J. Minford, Trans.). New York, NY: Penguin Books—Great Ideas.

Svara, J. H. (2014). *The ethics primer for public administrators in government and nonprofit organizations.* Burlington, MA: Jones & Bartlett Publishers.

Transparency International. (2011). *National integrity system: Background rationale and methodology*. Retrieved March 2, 2016 from: www.transparency.org/files/content/nis/NIS_Background_Methodology_EN.pdf

Uhr, J. (2015). *Prudential public leadership: Promoting ethics in public policy and administration*. Basingstoke, UK: Palgrave MacMillan.

Visser, H. (2016). Integrity incorporated in strategy and daily processes: The Netherlands Tax and Custom Administration. In Huberts, L., & Hoekstra, A. (Eds.), *Integrity management in the public sector: The Dutch approach* (pp. 146–158). The Hague: Bios.

Walzer, M. (1973). Political action: The problem of dirty hands. *Philosophy and Public Affairs, 2*(2), 160–179.

Weick, K. E. (1995). *Sensemaking in organizations* (Foundations for organizational science). Thousand Oak, CA: Sage Publications Inc.

Zimbardo, P. (2007). *The Lucifer effect: Understanding how good people turn evil*. New York, NY: Random House.

7 Value Driven Leading
Thinking in Multiple Dimensions

Managerial leaders can integrate the multiple ethical and political aspects of value driven leading by deploying a set of mental frames to focus decision making as individuals and teams. Practiced attention to these four dimensions in decision making creates a higher prospect of incorporating values and effectiveness in decisions. These dimensions combine the many lines of value and political analysis discussed in earlier chapters into a four-fold process of reflection. They generate preliminary checklists that people can use to focus their thinking. This approach begins with self-awareness and intentional thinking to address the major elements involved in striving for ethical, effective and sustainable organizational and policy results.

Individual managers and leaders can adopt this frame, practice using it and become proficient to deploy this approach as a normal frame to engage the challenges of managerial leading. Pausing to adopt this cognitive review and process helps managerial leaders ensure values and mission goals and guide decisions even as individuals attend to the dense political reality around them. It helps people align values with their long-term projects and forge durable outcomes. Projects that disappear the minute a leader leaves or looks away represent ethical and managerial failure. This framework requires leaders to attend to the prudent and effectiveness aspects of action as well as the upfront value and mission demands.

To achieve this type of consistent leadership as a manager, value driven leading encourages individuals to master these frames to guide judgement in a self-aware and recursive manner through four dimensions. These dimensions focus attention and guide assessment across four critical aspects of achieving integrity driven solutions. These dimensions are:

- Understand one's values, character and mission commitment
- Manage the meaning of organizational incidents or challenges
- Act to build long-term organizational norms and policy direction
- Secure the power and resources necessary for resilient outcomes.

In the daily flow of influencing policy and organizations, individuals can practice and train themselves and their teams to use these frames of judgment. These focused mental frames can be practiced and learned. They help people align cognition, emotion and perception to support physical action with deep and patterned neural processes. This framework builds upon the initial framework for public integrity in Chapter 3. It organizes and expands it to apply to daily and fine-grained decisions while keeping a strategic focus. The catalogue of reference points can discipline and direct reflection and point individuals to vital aspects they might miss without the checklists.

The neural networks support developed and trained intuitions that managerial leaders can quickly deploy to assess context and decide on action. One's trained perception reveals patterns of relevant ethical, political and organizational attributes with speed and cognitive efficiency. Managerial leaders can practice and train their minds to go through these dimensions in an iterative manner facing the unfolding incidents life presents. Working with a team can extend this shared disciplined thinking. This systematic reflection permits individuals to connect actions to their commitments and character. Using these frames guides people to direct responses to incidents to align with goals while building a power and resource base for the long term.

Self-aware individuals can intentionally go through each dimensions and cross check them to get solutions that align the four dimensions that should guide institutional leadership. Each dimension can be seen as a circle in a Venn diagram, and reflection seeks where they overlap. Each could be

Diagram 7.1 Value Driven Leading Framework

seen as lenses to look through, and each lens clarifies the political and ethical terrain and creates a more multi-dimensional ethical landscape in which to act. This process resembles recursive self-awareness to refine one's cognitive attention and judgment. They can become a regulated habit of trained reflection to focus individual and team attention.

Focal Points of Leading in Multiple Dimensions

- Maintain self-awareness
- Engage the meaning of incidents and challenges
- Build for long-term policy direction or organizational norms and culture
- Attend to the necessary power and resources for resilient outcomes

Maintain Self-Awareness

Political wisdom from the Delphic Oracle to Socrates to Sun Tzu has argued that knowing oneself is a critical linchpin of effective leadership ethics. Modern research reinforces this classic insight that the self-aware ability to step back and assess is vital to good leading. The window of self-awareness permits persons to recalibrate beliefs, scan political environments and adapt values to the context.

Self-awareness supports a managerial leader's quest to develop reliable judgment engaged with mission purpose and the challenges presented by a situation. A managerial leader with integrity needs to possess self-mastery that controls and integrates their emotions, cognitions and perceptions. This stance builds on personal responsibility where persons take control of internal actions to align cognitive capacity to master ideals, rules and goals. Each dimension generates a preliminary checklist that can guide a person's reflection and judgment. Self-assessment of this dimension involves:

- Accept responsibility for the position
- Know how one's values and character connect to mission
- Master oneself and stand back from pressures of the moment
- Know one's default frames of judgment and character tendencies
- Attend to and avoid cognitive and emotional traps
- Exercise disciplined openness to information and people
- Decide and act in contested political and organizational environments
- Strive to infuse daily action and culture with purpose and focus

Self-awareness provides a buffer against getting trapped into preexisting power arrangements and locked into de fault understandings of a situation. Humans are constantly tempted by confirmation bias, leading them to see and hear only what meets their own preconceptions. Many cognitive heuristics tempt people to prematurely close their understanding of a situation and narrow the information they take seriously or people they hear. Groupthink aggravates these tendencies to be trapped by narrow understandings of situations. Time pressures amplify the tendency to accept initial frame assessments and act. At the same time, individuals are tempted by self-deception or rationalization to avoid the dissonance and ethical pain of flawed and incomplete actions. Being self-aware, responsible and stepping back to deliberate avoids cognitive traps and enables leaders to adapt to new information and learn from others.

The importance of self-aware integrity grows in the domain of partnerships, contracting and collaboration. No one chain of accountability organizes action, and different organizational missions and interests pull in many directions. Self-awareness is critical to lead across the pull of different interests and ideological positions. The diverse stakeholders in partnerships and collaborations constantly seek to impose their understandings or interests onto cooperative endeavors. Contractors possess a wide array of incentives to maximize their own gains at the expense of the public purpose.

Managerial leading in these circumstances requires improvisation in light of surprises and endless divergent interests. Self-aware leaders need to weave together common understandings of a situation or forge shared interests. They must be willing to negotiate and when necessary enforce public purpose and accountability across stakeholders. This involves open-minded attention to the understandings and interests of stakeholders as well as careful attention to weak signals and ferreting out unknown unknowns to adapt to changes among cooperators, competitors and opponents.

A person's values and character activate through committing to the mission of the organization. The mission and outcomes mandated establish the deeper leadership and management task of cultivating an abiding sense of ethical purpose for the organization, groups and people. Purpose reveals itself as the intent that guides people performing tasks. Managers can achieve goals with sustained behavior and compliance among people. But their self-awareness gives them the leverage to nurture a sense of purpose and meaning in people's jobs that can drive personnel to perform at more consistent levels, take stewardship of goals more seriously and resist corruption more consistently.

Values and commitments manifest themselves in purpose and intent. An accepted purpose structures ethical intent, decision architecture and motivation for commitments. Leaders can model and drive a sense of purpose to suffuse daily tasks with intention, meaning and direction. Nurturing purpose in people and relations creates the deep structure that supports organizational culture, mission and goals.

Organizational purpose guides individual decisions best when they grow from strong knowledge of the mission, laws, codes and rules that guide work. The laws, regulations and processes are authorized means to achieve results. Mastering the deep-rooted purpose and knowledge also gives managers the ability to understand their discretion and exercise it resourcefully when rigid enforcement of rules can lead to unintended wrongs or denying responsibility will lead to pathological consequences.

Engage the Meaning of Incidents and Challenges

Having a value driven culture depends upon people sharing the same mental frames of reference that enable individuals to diagnose situations in a similar manner. Shared meaning builds trust across individuals and groups and provides common reference points to assess each other and outcomes. These shared understandings help people to make sense of the world they live in and anticipate other personnel's judgments and performance. Shared understandings build trust in each other's decisions, make communication more efficient and authority clearer. They smooth coordination across problems and organizational processes. Keeping control of the shared meanings for personnel especially during problematic moments becomes an ongoing leadership responsibility.

Organizational life presents managerial leaders with an endless array of decisions, most of which can be made upon the basis of trained judgment and internalized mental frames. These unfolding decisions depend upon common organizational norms and understandings and usually reinforce accepted organizational culture and goals. However, such normal progressions can miss structural or cultural problems hidden within an organization's normal patterns. These might involve systematic patterns of underperformance, discrimination, corruption, mini-empires of bullies or peer group norms that defend corrupt practice. They might also simply be inadequate for a surprise incident that arises.

Incidents disturb the normal flow of expected decisions and issues and occur on a regular and random basis. They demand a higher cognitive and emotional engagement by managers, but they present as "problems" when they threaten disruptions of the flow of meaning and practice within an organization. Managers might see underperformance or mistakes. Actors or stakeholders might claim that the organization or personnel have violated its rules or people have been mistreated in ways that violate organizational or social values. The conflict can be amplified by eruptions of verbal or behavioral anger and resistance. Each problem incident involves conflicts over the meaning of what occurred and how this impacts the culture of the organization. In a different vein, problems can lurk beneath the surface and require intense effort by managerial leaders to excavate issues or diagnose weak organizational signals than an incident might be sending. The disruption might reveal failures of performance that result in disastrous outcomes because of failed or corrupt regulation or performance in daily duties or be a flashpoint for group or client tensions. Any of these can be magnified by media intervention, internal investigations or stakeholder litigation.

All these challenges whether subterranean pathologies or sudden manifestations of failures of competence, performance or respect require serious attention from managerial leaders. The stakes of such incidents cascade out into the viability and meaning of the culture and its values and practices. Each action a manager takes to address incident problems sets a precedent that reverberates across the organization and defines expectations for the future. Cumulative action responses can build or undermine cultural or policy goals.

Being self-aware, knowing one's values and mission purpose as well as working to understand all the political and cultural implications of a situation involve hard ethical and mental work. The initial checklist for this dimension guides managers to:

- Remember long-term norms and culture goals
- Identify the different possible understandings of an event
- Understand the relevant actors and groups and their interests in controlling its meaning
- Search to uncover if the event reveals hidden or entrenched structural challenges
- Identify salient local aspects of a problem for mission achievement
- Influence the meaning of the unfolding incident
- Align any action to longer-term norms of organizational culture or policy

Whatever the incident, and however small, some protagonists will have different interpretations and agendas and will fight to control the meaning of an incident. While many people will be neutral and default to understandings based on history or their positions, some stakeholders will have agendas and interests, sometimes, at odds with the ethical direction of a managerial leader. They can use any incidents, even minor ones such as misperceived jokes, mistakes in allocation of resources, lost tempers or a small but disruptive ethical victory, to pursue their parochial aims or derail a leader's purposes.

An incident might also be symptomatic of deep-rooted problems such as corruption of an individual or unit or reflect the power of an informal bully or peer norms that subvert performance or accountability. Actors will rise to defend the inertia of the organization to protect their interests. Groups will argue an incident is only a "one off" or reflects just one bad apple; either approach creates narratives designed to end further scrutiny. Any managerial leader facing something that seems simple such as a misrepresented information, abusive client treatment or a negligent inspection confronts all these hidden possibilities. They have the option to address the problem as a regular incident or use it as a political window to investigate and initiate changes.

This means leaders need to work to control the perception and definition of problems or an incident. These meanings of the incident and solutions will influence the internal political and cultural intensity of support or opposition. This contest over the meaning of incidents or events impacts possible allies for building culture or a power base. Influencing how events and actions are perceived can affect bringing people on as collaborators or contribute to small victories that build credibility and momentum toward the leader's legitimacy and goals. The narrative around the event can cover up grave issues or open up new changes. There are no really small events that can be ignored if they have the potential to reveal or hide deeper conflict over purpose, performance and culture.

To build up reliable institutional purpose or policy implementation, leaders must work to shape the meaning of incidents to build a political understanding and organizational culture that supports reliable behavior connected to the purpose. Unless actively managed, the impact of peer pressure and informal authority over time can erode both a leader's self-confidence and autonomy and lead people to become acclimated to dangerous or ethically problematic behavior. The institutionalization of deviance relies upon managerial indifference or laziness around small issues and concealed meanings that can result in massive institutional failure and wrongdoing. Shaping the environment and culture become ethical imperatives, and leaders cannot rely solely upon individual behavior or individual virtue to achieve goals.

Build for the Long-Term Institution and Policy

Effective managerial leading is informed by stewardship and decides with an eye on momentum toward organizational results or policy for the long term. This longer focus should shape the ethical, political and organizational arc of actions. Each decision and each action cumulatively build out toward abiding goals. Keeping in mind the reverberations of actions outward to stakeholders and inward toward personnel strengthens decisions that might be subverted by short-term demands or interests. This process builds upon knowing one's values and mission and influencing the meaning of unfolding events. The personal reflective checklist covers:

- Know the political actors and stakeholders
- Uncover the hidden actors and unheard voices

- Plan for the long game
- Inform decisions with desired organizational norms and outcomes
- Be aware of setting precedents
- Manage ethical and behavioral boundaries
- Earn credibility and legitimacy
- Attend to long-term momentum for goals
- Monitor and learn from unanticipated consequences

Long-term achievement and stewardship depend upon a thorough and up-to-date awareness of the major political actors and stakeholder's in one's political environment. This world constantly evolves and deeply impacts lasting success or failure of a leader's initiatives. Knowing and mapping the actors begins the continuous process of identifying the critical actors for one's purposes and cultivating knowledge of and relationships with them in pursuit of organizational and policy goals. In mapping the political environment, managerial leaders who are committed to dignity and respect need to pay particular attention to identify and cultivate political actors who may not be well organized or powerful but may be deeply affected by the policies involved. These actors often represent the hidden victims of unanticipated consequences or the silent voices whose interests are overlooked. It becomes a positive obligation of public officials to ensure such hidden and overlooked actors are involved in the decisions.

The long game plays out through establishing a culture of commitment to high levels of performance and to the values imbedded in the mission of the organization. A culture can live with people's compliance, but to thrive it needs people's commitment. Staff and personnel achieve higher levels of performance, innovation and integrity when they connect their self-narratives and interests to the organization's purpose. A durable culture strengthens performance but also buttresses the ability to resist ethical slippage and corruption.

Reflective action in this dimension aims to generate stable mental frame formation among individuals, groups and institutions to support a culture of quality performance of goals. A leader's actions create signals, precedents, expectations, boundaries and incentives. They establish reputations and future possibilities, and managerial leaders need to be sure that these consequences support the character and goals they seek. Success in the long run involves resetting expectations, reconnecting individual's actions with purpose, building trust in the purpose and leader as well as trust in each other. Intentional actions shaped by consistent purpose and attention to the context and culture will accumulate impact over time.

Relentless and consistent dedication to a valued purpose, making hard decisions and following through on promises builds a leader's reputation and credibility. This is earned not just in daily actions but also critically in managing the boundaries of ethical and performance behavior. The bound-aries are pressed by personnel who subvert purposes, but also the boundar-ies are where external actors intrude to capture the organization for their purposes. Managers who tolerate underperformance or unethical behavior undermine their credibility and abet contagious underperformance and dis-trust among personnel and stakeholders. Building ethical and political capi-tal has to be factored in decisions given the grueling task of managing for an integrity-based culture. It takes courage and persistence to engage unac-ceptable behavior in the boundary lands, and doing so is hard and endur-ing work, but only these efforts can protect the integrity of the people and organization.

No action is perfect. No person is perfect. Certainly no organization is perfect. On a regular basis, managerial leaders will make mistakes. Unan-ticipated consequences will emerge from actions. New voices will identify overlooked harms. Lasting success and legitimacy depends upon being open and responsive to failures, mistakes and new knowledge of complex con-sequences. A commitment to personal and organizational learning requires honesty and transparency. It takes effort and discipline but pays out in better policies and processes as well as better allocation of resources and more impactful personnel. This reinforces self-awareness and intentional action for abiding purposes.

Building Power and Resources

Thinking through action for a managerial leader involves one more dimen-sion that ethics concerns often downplay. The obligations of office entail making a genuine difference—achieving results that endure. Durable and resilient results require prudent attention to finding resources to effect results and secure the power to implement and defend results against oppo-sition and attrition.

Public ethics often underplays the importance and necessity of power and resources. But creating solutions that evanesce before opposition or the friction of organizational politics constitutes ethical negligence. Even "victories" that seem firm only exist for a while as other goals arise, inertia reestablishes itself or opponents regroup; every sustained solution involves protracted effort.

No organization or policy exists without facing resistance or opposition both internally and externally. This can be as benign as inertia that misses emergent challenges, differences over the interpretation of a mandate or differences over priorities for limited resources. It can be impersonal where stakeholders view the resources and energy spent on a mission as an oppor-tunity cost to their own organization or policy. It might involve the pull of different mission driven organizations or different sectors trying to cooperate in achieving a goal. Or it might involve simple and direct opposition to the organization's mission or to proposed changes in the purpose of a group, unit or organization.

A wide array of power and support exist throughout organizations. Resources ranging from intellectual capital to physical structures to technologies to partners to procedures or budgets exist in abundance. Integrating these considerations into managerial leading involves imagination, endless negotiation and a practiced awareness of the evolving context and opportunities. The preliminary checklist to guide managerial leading about resources and power starts with:

- Build one's authority and credibility
- Know the relevant political actors and stakeholders
- Attend to timing and windows of opportunity
- Connect actions to people's beliefs and interests
- Practice reciprocity for the long term
- Contribute to the legitimacy of oneself and the organization
- Create networks of supporters aligned by belief and interest
- Align networks and critical relationships to sustain monetary support
- Build relationships for protracted politics
- Foster a culture of performance and commitment as a resource
- Invest in constant listening, communication and media planning

Managerial leaders need a constant focus on their ability to induce individuals and groups to support actions or defend achievements against efforts to subvert or defund them. This begins with building the power and credibility of their own positional responsibilities, however, innocuous it may seem. Good leaders are always building out their influence through achievement, follow-through, and trusted connections as well as their willingness to help others accomplish their goals. They often give help to others across a wide array of purposes and organizations, sometimes with no real demand for reciprocation. Their presence can generate a predictable array of motives: respecting authority, acting on trust, acknowledging past relationships, acting in anticipation of future benefits, acting from commitment to the mission or simply out of duty to their job. This approach builds a network of connection, obligation and trust across a wide array of political and organizational actors. These strong and weak connections can be mobilized to support positions of the managerial leader. Just as important, managerial leaders must possess the power and willingness to impose adverse consequences on people to manage boundaries, create credibility and trust, and address threats to the organization and policy.

Building and deploying power well requires a constant attention to the relevant actors and stakeholders in a leader's political environment. Managerial leaders must constantly scan their authorizing and funding environments and develop relations with the institutional authorizers that impact their organization's legitimacy and resources. This attention to the constellations of power and interest as well as actors who may be unrepresented gives power a strategic cast. Networks of shared interest in outcomes as well as shared belief in purpose can evoke stronger and more resilient support than simple reciprocity, fear of consequences or deference to authority. Developing and deepening these webs of power and reliance build upon patterns of giving, attention, listening, responsiveness as well as integrity-based relationships and performance over time.

Establishing connections with collaborators or allies involves never-ending negotiations and compromises to cultivate shared commitments even as distance in networks and local conditions constrain beliefs and actions. Sometimes keeping momentum alive or minimizing mortal harm to the institution becomes the best that can be achieved. This dimension points leaders to pursue support, legitimacy and resources that possess political resilience.

Exercising initiative involves not just scanning for power and resources but also a constant awareness of timing and opportunity. Good managerial leaders take advantage of windows of opportunity to initiate larger changes or take on structural challenges. Elections, changes of regimes, new leaders and significant failures all pose opportunities to probe for change. A politically attuned leader can turn even innocuous events into political leverage points. Leaders need to address incidents in a strategic way to ensure continuous learning and progress toward culture and goals. Most impactful incidents begin with a contest to define its meaning, and few issues arrive with interpretations baked in. Leaders need to attend to not just internal but also external meanings and to changes in funding, budgets, elections, economic cycles or new agendas to refine their own initiatives.

Political power is required to gain substantial resources to sustain organizational or unit performance. The ability to maintain monetary support from authorizers, funders and clients must always be part of calculations. Acquiring and training for the best available technologies is critical in times of budgetary stringency and to offset the inequalities in power often facing public organizations. In addition, a strong culture committed to performance and integrity becomes a bulwark of power and resource against the headwinds of opposition, corruption or asymmetric interests and power. The culture, itself, depends upon acquiring appropriate technologies, internal controls and reliable expertise coupled with adequate compensation and physical resources.

Protracted efforts to build organizations of performance and integrity in evolving political environments requires constant investment in listening, communication and media. Attention and listening permits managerial leaders to anticipate emerging issues and conflicts and to connect with concerns of stakeholders and personnel. Adaptable and mutual communication enables leaders to constantly remind and reinforce relationships with authorizers, personnel, partners, allies and stakeholders of the purpose and advantages of actions and support. The communication also continuously builds culture and legitimacy. At the same time communication is linked to purpose and incident management. Durable results require cultivating all available means of communication and listening and building sustained multiple channel media communication plans.

A managerial leader alone or with a team can develop the reliable practice of addressing iteratively each of these four dimensions. They let the dimensions test each other and react back, influence and reach balance across their concerns. This recursive reflection helps leaders to address each of the four dimensions of action and accomplishment over time and informs each decision with purpose, meaning, direction and capability.

Bibliography

Applbaum, A. I. (1999). *Ethics for adversaries: The morality of roles in public and professional life.* Princeton, NJ: Princeton University Press.

Badaracco, J. (1997). *Defining moments.* Cambridge, MA: Harvard Business School Press.

Badaracco, J. (2002). *Leading quietly: An unorthodox guide to doing the right thing.* Cambridge, MA: Harvard Business Press.

Badaracco, J. (2016). Managing yourself: How to tackle your toughest decisions. *Harvard Business Review,* 104–107.

Bardach, E., & Kagan, R. A. (1982). *Going by the book: The problem of regulatory unreasonableness.* Philadelphia, PA: Temple University Press.

Bazerman, M. H., & Tenbrunsel, A. E. (2011). *Blind spots: Why we fail to do what's right and what to do about it.* Princeton, NJ: Princeton University Press.

Bertok, J. et al. (2005). *Public sector integrity: A framework for analysis.* Paris, France: OECD.

Bolman, L. G., & Deal, T. E. (2011). *Reframing organizations: Artistry, choice and leadership.* New York, NY: John Wiley & Sons.

Bryson, J., Crosby, B., & Bloomberg, L. (Eds.). (2015). *Creating public value in practice: Advancing the common good in a multi-sector, shared power, no-one-wholly-in-charge-world.* Boca Raton, FL: Taylor & Francis Group.

Carter, S. L. (1996). *Integrity.* New York, NY: Basic Books.

Christensen, C. M., Allworth, J., & Dillon, K. (2012). *How will you measure your life?* New York, NY: Harper Collins.

Cohen, S., & Eimicke, W. (2002). *The effective public manager: Achieving success in a changing government* (3rd. edition). San Francisco, CA: Jossey-Bass.

Cooper, T. L., & Wright, N. D. (Eds.). (1992). *Exemplary public administrators: Character and leadership in government.* San Francisco, CA: Jossey-Bass.

Crick, B. (1972). *In defence of politics* (2nd edition). Chicago, IL: University of Chicago Press.

Dobel, J. P. (1990). *Compromise and political action: Political morality in liberal and democratic life.* Savage, MD: Rowman & Littlefield.

Dobel, J. P. (1990). Integrity in the public service. *Public Administration Review, 50*(3), 354–367.

Dobel, J. P. (1998). Political prudence and the ethics of leadership. *Public Administration Review, 58*(1), 74–81.

Dobel, J. P. (1999). *Public integrity.* Baltimore, MD: Johns Hopkins University Press.

Dobel, J. P. (2005). Managerial leadership and the ethical importance of legacy. *International Public Management Journal, 8*(2), 225–246.

Dobel, J. P. (2007). Public management as ethics. In Ferlie, E., Lynn, Jr., L. E., & Pollitt, C. (Eds.), *The Oxford handbook of public management* (pp. 156–181). Oxford, UK: Oxford University Press.

Gawande, A. (2010). *Checklist manifesto.* New York, NY: Penguin Books.

Goldhamer, H. (1978). *The advisor.* New York, NY: Elsevier.

Goodsell, C. (2011). *The mission mystique: Belief systems in public agencies.* Washington, DC: CQ Press.

Gracian, B. (1993). *The art of worldly wisdom* (C. Maurer, Trans.). New York, NY: Doubleday.

Graycar, A., & Prenzler, T. (2013). *Understanding and preventing corruption.* Basingstoke, UK: Palgrave Macmillan.

Janis, I. L. (1982). *Groupthink: Psychological studies of policy decisions and fiascoes.* Boston, MA: Houghton Mifflin.

Janis, I. L., & Mann, L. (1977). *Decision making: A psychological analysis of conflict, choice, and commitment.* New York, NY: Free Press.

Jurkiewicz, C. L. (2006). Power and ethics: The communal language of effective leadership. In Frederickson, H. G., & Ghere, R. K. (Eds.), *Ethics in public management* (pp. 95–113). Armonk, NY: M. E. Sharpe.

Kahneman, D. (2011). *Thinking, fast and slow.* New York, NY: Macmillan.

Kaplan, R. S., & Norton, D. P. (2004). *Strategy maps: Converting intangible assets into tangible outcomes.* Cambridge, MA: Harvard Business Press.

Klein, G. A. (1998). *Sources of power: How people make decisions.* Cambridge, MA: MIT Press.

Klein, G. A. (2009). *Streetlights and shadows: Searching for the keys to adaptive decision making.* Cambridge, MA: MIT Press.

Klitgaard, R. R. (1991). *Controlling corruption.* Berkeley, CA: University of California Press.

Klitgaard, R. R., MacLean-Abaroa, R., & Parris, H. L. (2000). *Corrupt cities: A practical guide to cure and prevention.* Oakland, CA: Institute of Contemporary Studies Press.

Kornblum, A. N. (1976). *Moral hazards: Police strategies for honesty and ethical behavior*. Lexington, MA: Lexington Books.

Moore, M. M. (1995). *Creating public values: Strategic management in government*. Cambridge, MA: Harvard University Press.

O'Leary, R., & Bingham, L. B. (Eds.). (2009). *The collaborative public manager: New ideas for the twenty-first century*. Washington, DC: Georgetown University Press.

Rawls, J. (1971). *A theory of justice*. Cambridge, MA: Belknap Press of Harvard University Press.

Rose-Ackerman, S. (2013). *Corruption: A study in political economy*. New York, NY: Academic Press.

Rose-Ackerman, S., & Palifka, B. J. (2016). *Corruption and government: Causes, consequences, and reform*. Cambridge, UK: Cambridge University Press.

Rotberg, R. I. (2017). *The corruption cure: How citizens and leaders can combat graft*. Princeton, NJ: Princeton University Press.

Sabato, L. J. (1991). *Feeding frenzy: Attack journalism in American politics*. New York, NY: The Free Press.

Schein, E. H. (2009). *The corporate culture survival guide*. San Francisco, CA: Jossey-Bass.

Schein, E. H. (2010). *Organizational culture and leadership*. New York, NY: John Wiley & Sons.

Schon, D. (1984). *The reflective practitioner: How professionals think in action*. New York, NY: Basic Books.

Sun-tzu. (2006). *The art of war* (J. Minford, Trans.). New York, NY: Penguin Books—Great Ideas.

The European Ombudsman. (2003). *The European code for good administrative behavior*. Luxemburg: Office for Publications of the European Communities.

Thompson, D. F. (1980). Moral responsibility in government: The problem of many hands. *American Political Science Review, 74*, 905–916.

Thompson, D. F. (1987). *Political ethics and public office*. Cambridge, MA: Harvard University Press.

Thompson, D. F. (2005). *Restoring responsibility: Ethics in government, business, and healthcare* (Vol. 575). Cambridge, UK: Cambridge University Press.

Uhr, J. (2015). *Prudential public leadership: Promoting ethics in public policy and administration*. Basingstoke, UK: Palgrave MacMillan.

Walzer, M. (1973). Political action: The problem of dirty hands. *Philosophy and Public Affairs, 2*(2), 160–179.

Weick, K. E. (1995). *Sensemaking in organizations* (Foundations for organizational science). Thousand Oak, CA: Sage Publications Inc.

Conclusion

Ethics in organizations is not just about the personal integrity and behavior of one individual. Few individuals even of great virtue can stand against the pervasive cognitive and emotional influences of group and situational pressure on integrity. Unethical and corrupt behaviors can swamp the best of persons. Individual ethical lapses can be just that—individual lapses—but more often they are symptoms of deeper problems in the culture and structure of an organization. For this reason, the importance of ethical leadership cascades far beyond the efforts of individuals to act with integrity as managerial leaders. Their efforts to act with integrity, model behavior and resist temptations flow into building networks and teams of committed individuals who share common purpose and unite their diverse talents and identities into a public purpose.

Ethical leadership rests on consistent and self-aware scrutiny and modeling by senior management coupled with the courage and competence of the midlevel managers and supervisors. Managers and supervisors bear the brunt of the front line work and problems. Managerial leaders and supervisors carry the culture of the organization and fight the daily battle for a just, humane and competent work environment. They draw upon the range of organizational leadership values from working for responsibility, competence, transparency and accountability to inclusion and stewardship of the long-term mission and legitimacy of the organization.

This book presents recurring inventories and checklists of ethical resources to focus a person's reflection on management activity. Its appendices present a set of skills and behaviors that managerial leaders can cultivate in themselves and their people. These skills become focal points to develop mental frames to guide attention and judgment. These skills help focus managerial attention upon doable personal and organizational behaviors. The skills and behaviors can guide personal and organizational reflection and focus individual and group attention to achieve high-performing organizations that are animated by powerful values that provide motivation, support and guidance to individuals. The checklists and inventories can frame the agenda to bring leadership teams together. These skills involve the consistent activity necessary to align the Mission/Person/Task triangle for each person with the institutional, political and cultural means to achieve their goals.

Integrating ethics into managing and leading can be achieved in many ways. The key is to identify the importance of the values and character traits necessary to achieve the behaviors required by the mission and weave them into the understanding of situations and decisions. This requires being aware of the ethical dimensions of persons, decisions and institutions. It also requires seeing the connection between ethics, building culture, institutional design and power base. Value driven leading requires seeing and communicating the connection between ethics and the mission outcomes. This approach is strengthened by attention to the range of unethical behavior and ethical slippage and strategic ways to address them.

Integrating ethics into managerial leading depends upon individual self-reflection. Personal self-awareness connects to developing integrated and shared frames of judgment that foster culture and communication based upon values. A person's self-awareness helps individuals to pause and stand back from their own cognitive frames and recognize their values, character and commitments as well as the obligations of the position they promise to take on. Self-awareness needs time and relationships beyond the scope of work to ensure its openness and honesty. It identifies the roles that ethics plays in organizations from anchoring mission and discretion to imbuing culture and motivation. The act of reflection claims personal responsibility and constructs personal integrity, and integrity anchors the ethical capacity to control one's inner emotional and cognitive life and act with intent and promise to achieve a mission.

Intentional reflection draws upon the wide array of moral resources available to a public managerial leader. Consciousness of values, character and culture as well as threats to integrity help individuals fit the right ethical interventions with the requirements of unfolding incidents and political challenges. The entire ethical stance of a managerial leader grows from the reality that managers lead every day as they model build culture, ensure competence and protect clients, citizens and vulnerable populations. Their leading secures the common purpose and capacity of an organization's mission.

Appendix
Skill and Behaviors for Value Driven Leading

Skill: Develop a Self-Awareness of One's Values and Character

Come to a self-conscious awareness of the values that individuals hold most deeply and actually use them to guide decisions and give narrative coherence to one's life. Come to an awareness of the basic emotional, psychological and physical dispositions that recur in daily life and help sustain decision and action.

Behaviors

- Have a clear sense of the values that provide coherence and meaning to one's life.
- Gain a clear awareness of the dispositions and character traits that are the regular and predictable dispositions and attributes that a person reveals on a daily basis and under stress.
- Become aware of the main frames of reference that a person is educated or socialized into and unconsciously resorts to in daily decisions.
- Discover one's learning styles, emotional intelligence levels and other relevant attributes that modern assessments can help bring to self-knowledge.
- Understand the default frames and emotional and ethical reactions that one will resort to in order to avoid being trapped by frames that do not match the requirements of a position or situation.
- Develop a short and usable personal mission statement that can be remembered and used in real life situations. Revise it on a regular basis.

Skill: Use the Self-Awareness as a Source of Leading and Managing

Reflect upon actions and actively work to learn from decisions. Be alert to not only the expression of values and character in decisions but also how they affect relationships and are perceived as model behavior. Be alert to where actions are misconstrued or failed to achieve desired results, and be open to learning and growing.

Behaviors

- Work to ensure an alignment between the mission and the daily expressed values of an organization and one's lived commitments.
- Identify where tensions and discontinuities exist between personal commitments and the demands of the organization and monitor them carefully to address the potential for self-deception, burn out or cynicism.
- Make staff aware of one's preferred styles of deciding, relating and acting.
- Learn how one best processes criticism and feedback. Communicate this and resist one's own defensiveness facing feedback.
- Work to be aware of staff's own frames of judgment and communication to minimize misunderstandings.
- Hire to complement and extend one's range of knowledge and skills, and provide emotional, intellectual and character balance among colleagues and teams.
- Make sure to develop a network of relationships, which can be professional or personal, to provide sources of honest, critical support and feedback.

Skill: Articulate the Values and Virtues of the Institution

Articulate the foundational values of the group or organization and build systems that sustain them throughout the group or organization. Know the values that undergird the mission of the group, organization, network or coalition; know the standards of professional action; and understand the relevant legal and institutional rules that authorize action.

Behaviors

- Articulate, communicate and model the values and behaviors expected.
- Possess and act consistently upon a clear sense of the foundational values and the real purpose of the organization.
- Constantly communicate the values by actions, words and consistently managing boundaries to encourage good behavior.
- Create a consistent communication strategy at all levels of the organization for the values and purposes of the organization.
- Work to help others see the connection between their own values and the values and actions of the organization.
- Help people see the moral worth of their duties and tasks.

- Do not let the mission statement become a dead letter.
- Know the applicable professional Codes of Ethics and expected standards of discretion for positions.
- Be patient but tenacious in changing the culture and building values, behaviors and networks of supporters.
- When uncertain refer to the resources available. Consult codes, superiors, human resources, legal affairs, ethics officers, outside networks or the Inspector General's Office.

Skill: Ensure That Leaders and Managers Embody the Norms of the Organization

Follow up the articulation of values and virtues with strong and consistent policy and actions that support, encourage and reward the values and character, but set limits and discipline upon expected behavior.

Behaviors

- Hire, promote, reward, draw boundaries and evaluate with an eye to the values of the organization.
- Define the expected rules and standards in behavioral terms to achieve fuller understanding, agreement and consistency.
- Make sure everyone learns and relearns the basic rules and standards.
- Consistently communicate the rules, standards and codes of ethics to personnel, colleagues and team members and judge performance accordingly.
- Model and demand that all supervisory personnel and team leaders model the values, virtues and behaviors required of the organization's mission.
- Create rituals and public occasions to recognize and celebrate the expected values, virtues and behaviors.
- Ensure that different points of view and hidden discrimination are surfaced and addressed in the values and behaviors.
- Manage conflict to remind individuals of the common values and the importance of respect in communicating and resolving tensions across persons and groups.
- Have the courage to defend the boundaries and requirements of the values.
- Provide a disciplinary path that permits individuals to grow into values and behaviors expected by the ethical purposes of the organization.
- Have the strength to follow through on discipline to define basic value and character behaviors.

Skill: Create Strong Support and Accountability for Ethics

Model values and character but also provide the right alignment of incentives and disincentives as well as holistic organizational supports needed to sustain norms and patterns of accountability. Provide the support needed by individuals who seek to act ethically.

Behaviors

- Understand one's own responsibilities and discretion.
- Define people's responsibilities and make them part of setting expectations, learning and managing on a daily basis.
- Avoid the temptation to deny responsibility and become too rigid, and address rule bound rigidity in others and oneself.
- Make sure good and bad behaviors have real consequences, even across teams, organizations and networks, in order to sustain the common values and recognition of accountability and purpose.
- Build team cohesion around commitment to the values and work hard to build in respect across individuals, expertise and groups.
- Recruit, hire and promote to ensure diverse points of view and talent pools are represented within the organization.
- Work relentlessly to understand peer norms, especially at the point of task performance, and inculcate support and behaviors for core organizational values.
- Be open to adapt required behaviors that flow from values in light of circumstances, changed mandates and resource limitations.
- In building new expectations, do not just identity the negatives; provide clear and sustained support and feedback on the right behaviors. Be consistent and sustained in this—it takes time.
- Build values expectations into performance evaluation.
- Be open to community involvement to understand, revise and support core values and performance.
- Understand when actions arise from good intent and are mistakes in discretion, not malfeasance. Remember, building a long-term culture requires staff to internalize and be proud of their value orientation.
- Have the courage and build the support to set clear boundaries for unacceptable behavior, and address unethical or illegal behavior in a fair and decisive manner.

Skill: Be Open to Learning From Others and Provide the Means for Effective Two-Way Engagement to Occur

Work on a personal style that invites candid conversation and feedback, and model a learning style that addresses mistakes as a chance to learn and grow. Create means through which individuals can effectively dissent, engage in helping the organization get better and safely identify problems and illegalities.

Behaviors

- Know one's learning styles and be aware of the strengths but also limits of one's normal framework. This self-awareness helps to adapt and learn from multiple points of view.
- Be alert to adapt required or traditional behaviors that flow from values to new circumstances, changed mandates and unanticipated consequences.
- Be open to community input into revising behaviors to adapt to mission purposes.
- Cultivate active listening to individuals, diverse groups and communities. Do not ask for candid feedback and then either ignore it or respond in anger, defensiveness or with perceived reprisals.
- Engage, reward and act upon solid, active dissent and candid insight.
- Communicate and build around mistakes by providing clear knowledge of the problem, modeling and practicing correct behaviors and supporting the right behavior consistently.
- Build in safe methods and places for individuals to report illegal, unethical or dangerous behavior. Have the courage to support and protect those individuals and systems.
- Have appropriate whistleblower mechanisms and protections for reporting that individuals can use safely when they fear reprisal from superiors.
- Actively listen to community and partner insights and integrate them into assessments of personnel and unanticipated consequences of organizational action.

Skill: Build a Culture of Cooperation and Commitment Among Staff, Colleagues, Collaborators and Management Teams

Modern governance requires cooperation with extended internal and external networks of collaborators, contractors and internal groups and units. Creating a sustained understanding of common purpose across these multiple groupings is one of the most effective and challenging means of ethical leading.

Behaviors

- Model and train with direct reference to values.
- Listen, dialogue and communicate to create a shared vocabulary of values and purposes. Attend to this constantly.
- Set a tone for colleagues and a group that creates a secure and candid environment to discuss values and ethical issues.
- Work to create cooperation and team successes by recognizing and rewarding actions that reflect the team's values, and encourage cooperative actions.
- Understand that each organization in collaborative endeavors will have their own divergent interests and understandings, and work to comprehend these and acknowledge them.
- Identify critical actors in each group who can become the focal point of communication and dissemination of common purposes.
- Give individuals and groups opportunities for input and initiative.
- Share credit generously.
- Work to ensure that individuals across stakeholders and collaborators are identified and brought respectfully into the deliberations about common purposes and implementation actions.
- Quickly address interpersonal issues of respect and perceptions of discrimination when they arise. Get help if needed.

Skill: Understand the Full Context of Incidents and Act Accordingly

Always remember the constant temptation to rely upon an individual's or group's preferred default framework for processing information and significance. Develop the strategic pause and, if given time, do not fall back upon default frameworks to react to a situation. Use self-awareness to step back, analyze the event, be open to diverse or multiple frames of analysis and trace the multiple environmental factors that influence a situation.

Behaviors

- Pause before responding instantly.
- Remember not every "incident" carries just one meaning. Work hard to both understand the multiple meanings people attach to the incident and create a common understanding that is fair but also attuned to the mission and values of the organizations.
- Map out the other stakeholders or diverse actors and understand their points of view and how they perceive the stakes and interests of understanding a situation.

- Engage each incident as a challenge to define it in a way that contributes to the emergence of mission norms and the desired long-term culture or policy goals.
- Work hard to identify and understand the subcultures and informal norms of an organization. Understand how these norms and subcultures influence definitions of an "incident" and use the incident as a chance to help educate or move the subcultures to support the mission.
- Monitor and address the boundary lands between the subcultures or different sets of informal norms. Pay close attention to boundary lands where different demographic or cultural groups contact each other. This can range from different professional groups to racial or gender groups. Address the latent tensions and advantages that flow from having diverse cultures as well as where they face off at an institutional boundary.
- Work hard to identify the diversity aspects of an incident. Anticipate these tensions in long-term managing, hiring and promoting, and ensure that the decision makers attend to it. Work to build not just training but reinforcing teams and actions to engage inclusion and integrate diverse people into the mission. Clarify the intent of the stakeholders when issues involving respect and perceived discrimination arise.
- Act decisively when the issues are clear to defend the values of inclusion, and align them with mission performance. Work to include communities, diverse people and frameworks into discussions and development of policy and action.
- Know the personal attributes of staff and understand their strengths and weaknesses. Support the growth of strengths and work to address weaknesses.

Skill: Anticipate Predictable Points of Vulnerability and Ethical Slippage

Map out the points of tension between value and performance that individuals experience on the job. Be alert to external and internal groups that have interests that would drive them to try to capture or subvert groups and individuals. Anticipate the pressures that can subvert the values and performance of individuals or teams and invest attention and resources to shore them up. Map out mismatches between resources, expectations or support, and external pressure or mismatches between internal and external stakes. Identity subcultures and contagion that subvert mission values.

Behaviors

- Understand when an organization possesses sole or exclusive power to provide vital services or regulate high stakes resources.

- Work to ensure that individuals at the point of task performance have the integrity, expertise, training, support, assets and technology to shore up the level of discretion they possess.
- Understand the places where greater oversight, clearer expectations or monitoring is needed to offset the levels of training, integrity or resources relative to the internal and external demands placed upon individuals performing tasks.
- Spend time and effort to identify the peer norms for groups performing tasks. Identify subcultures of organization and be alert to areas where external actors or dominant internal actors influence the peer norms of performance.
- Always monitor the relative resources given to a group compared to their expected level of performance. Evaluate goals and measures to ensure they are reasonable and that enough support exists to achieve them.
- Be alert to changes over time in a group's composition or challenges from the environment that may not match the group's demographic, capacity or training.
- Know where the pressure points emerge where external actors have high stakes and are motivated to influence staff or officials to get their way.
- Know the boundary areas where groups of different classes, gender, races, ethnicities or training encounter one another in an organizational context. Aggressively intervene to provide the training, support and personnel practices to guide the tensions into productive mission performance.
- Develop multiple and strong paths of information and accountability. Get out, walk around, engage the community impacted by organizations and create redundant reporting to identify where the boundaries between organization and environment are porous and impact internal norms.

Skill: Address Points of Vulnerability and Slippage

Take actions that review performance and outcomes to ensure they comport with mission and that resources align with the tasks and measures. Build support for cultural norms and engage in timely and appropriate oversight.

Behaviors

- Let individuals know that management has their back when they face efforts to subvert their integrity and performance.
- Search out signals or behaviors that could point to hidden unethical or corrupt behaviors or subcultures that could hide and enable unethical patterns.

- Ensure proper monitoring and accountability of task groups and immediately bring to bear extra attention or oversight when hints of underperformance or value slippage appear.
- Set and enforce clear and consistent boundaries with respect to prohibited behavior.
- Bring to bear resources, support, training and engagement in areas to build up the integrity, expertise and resource base of people performing tasks under internal and external pressure that can undermine performance.
- Acknowledge honestly the issues and challenges personnel face and turn them into collective goals to which all can contribute.
- Provide positive paths for individuals and groups to move beyond ethical slippage and challenges.
- Celebrate and reward the successes and improvements against ethical and performance challenges.
- Provide sufficient training for individuals in their jobs so they are confident in making decisions.
- When introducing new technologies work to provide sufficient resources to train staff, build in buffers to transition time and monitor for slippages in performance.
- Work to win over influential informal actors to the values and expectations of the organization.
- Act quickly to avoid contagion and downward cycles when ethical slippage is identified. Get help when needed to address the vulnerabilities as soon as reasonable.

Index